281939

D1644378

Creating a learning to learn school

Toby Greany
& Jill Rodd

**research and practice for raising standards,
motivation and morale**

CAMPAIGN FOR **LEARNING**

Published by Network Educational Press Ltd
P O Box 635
Stafford
ST16 1BF

© Campaign for Learning 2003

ISBN 1 85539 186 4

Managing Editor: Martha Harrison
Design and layout: Neil Hawkins, NEP
Mind maps: Neil Hawkins, NEP
Illustrations on p. 47, 54, 58 and 71: Shelle Pugh
Poster: Kerry Ingham
Printed by MPG Books Ltd., Bodmin, Cornwall.

Contents

Acknowledgements

This book would not have been written without the help and support of many people and organizations, most importantly the heads and their teams whose hard work and dedication is described throughout. In addition to thanking them we would like to thank:

The project's patrons: Professor Tim Brighouse, Sir John Daniel, Professor Susan Greenfield and Professor David Hargreaves.

The project's advisory board: John Abbott, Dr Javier Bajer, Sir Christopher Ball, Tom Bentley, Dr Chris Brookes, Tony Buzan, Jose Chambers, Professor Guy Claxton, Galina Dolya, Neil Dunnicliffe, Maggie Farrah, Dr Peter Honey, Jim Houghton, Lesley James, Professor Elizabeth Leo, Dr Bill Lucas, Dr Juliet Merrifield, Roger Opie, Colin Rose, Judy Sebba, Alistair Smith, Lady Mary Tovey, Ray Wicks and Kate Williamson.

To our major sponsors, the Esmée Fairbairn Foundation, the Lifelong Learning Foundation, Accelerated Learning Systems Ltd and NfER Nelson, we are especially grateful, as we are to all those other organizations which have supported us along the way: Alite, Brain Trust, Comino Foundation, Design Council, Lloyds TSB, National Grid plc, the University of the First Age and, of course, our publishers, Network Educational Press.

Foreword

I welcome this report for the evidence it provides of the impact of 'learning to learn' approaches on raising standards, pupil motivation and teacher morale. All three are top priorities for this government. I also welcome the challenge it provides to make stronger links between schooling and lifelong learning. The 'learning to learn' skills that pupils develop in the schools in this project, such as reasoning, problem-solving and self-assessment, are those needed to be effective learners throughout adulthood. Learning skills are key for survival in the twenty-first century and I am delighted that this project is continuing to explore ways in which they can best be developed.

The report draws out the central importance of leadership in schools to set high expectations, monitor progress and motivate pupils and staff. Within the national literacy, numeracy and Key Stage 3 strategies, leadership is now a major focus and together with the National College for School Leadership, the government is investing significant resources in developing school leaders for the future. Leaders of the schools in this project demonstrate *instructional leadership* in which their main energy focuses on teaching and learning. These schools are also characterized by collaboration and use of data. The staff and pupils are involved in collecting and analysing information on their progress and using this to inform future priorities. They work with other schools to share ideas, expertise and resources.

The project schools supported by the Campaign for Learning have done a good job in co-ordinating this initiative. I hope headteachers, teachers and teaching assistants will read it. I am pleased that the Department is supporting the next phase of the project and look forward to hearing further reports of the progress.

David Miliband, MP
Minister of State for School Standards
Department for Education and Skills

Why 'learning to learn' is important for heads and schools

Leadership and learning are indispensable to each other.

John F. Kennedy

At the opening of the National College for School Leadership in October 2002, Professor Leo Tan, Director of the National Institute of Education in Singapore, closed his presentation with this quotation. It was a moving message, reminding us that the issues leaders face across the boundaries of space and time and that we who work as professional educators are not unique in our concern for learning.

Most of the technology that middle-aged people use routinely at work and home did not exist when they were at school. We cannot imagine the skills and knowledge that today's five year olds will need when they start work. They will learn as they go, just as we have, but because the pressures of change will probably be even greater for them, we need to do a better job of preparing them.

The Campaign for Learning have pulled together research from relevant fields of psychology, cognitive science and technology to enable a group of case study schools to put 'learning to learn' into practice. It is fascinating reading. There is certainly no silver bullet here, but there are plenty of ideas on which schools can draw to enhance the learning potential of their pupils.

From the start, the National College for School Leadership has put learning at the heart of the leadership agenda. That means that leaders must learn continuously and develop their schools as professional learning communities in which the capacity of staff and pupils alike is enhanced through collaborative learning.

This kind of learning agenda requires a different leadership approach. Power and authority need to be distributed so that ideas spring up and are developed in many different ways by many different people. The head's challenge is to bind these individual initiatives and energies together in a unifying vision and to build the trust that empowers teachers to learn alongside their pupils.

Creating a learning to learn school is far more than a teachers' tool-kit. It has the potential to make us all more self-aware as learners and challenges us to broaden and deepen our repertoire of learning strategies. Those who claim to lead learning organizations have a responsibility to model the behaviour they advocate. We have to be seen to give time to our learning, to be prepared to move out of our comfort zone, to value feedback, to be capable of changing our behaviour. Leading learning is a tough business.

Heather Du Quesnay
Director and Chief Executive
National College for School Leadership
February 2003

Introduction

Creating a learning to learn school is a book for heads, senior managers and teachers interested in developing better schools, classrooms and learners. It is based on two years of ground-breaking research in 25 schools by over a hundred teachers and many thousands of pupils. The research explored a variety of approaches to teaching pupils how they learn and evaluated the impact of these approaches on standards, pupil motivation and teacher morale.

Creating a learning to learn school sets out:

- why 'learning to learn' is important today
- the implications of 'learning to learn' for the government's educational reforms
- what we mean by 'learning to learn'
- the findings from the 'learning to learn' research project
- how heads and teachers can develop 'learning to learn' in their own schools.

Throughout the book, case studies based on the research projects and findings of individual schools are included, along with resources for auditing and developing 'learning to learn' in your school and helpful summaries of key research and the different learning approaches that make up 'learning to learn'. The research findings themselves in Chapter 5 are presented as photocopiable sheets for use in staff INSET, as are the audit questionnaires.

Also included is a colour poster for use in classrooms setting out what is involved in 'learning to learn' for pupils.

Related publications

- *Learning to learn: setting an agenda for schools in the 21st century* (Bill Lucas and Toby Greany; Campaign for Learning. Network Educational Press, 2001) sets out the original thinking behind the project.

- *Teaching pupils how to learn: research, practice and INSET resources* (Bill Lucas, Toby Greany, Jill Rodd and Ray Wicks; Campaign for Learning, Network Educational Press, 2002) sets out the findings from the first year of the research and is aimed at a general teaching audience.

- Separate research reports by Dr Jill Rodd covering years one and two of the project are available from the Campaign's website www.campaign-for-learning.org.uk. The research findings and case studies included in this book are taken from the Phase 2 Project Research Report.

Before you start reading...

Cast your mind back to your own earliest memory of learning something. Was it formal, like learning to spell your name, or informal, like learning that your older siblings always won in the end?

What about your first memory of using a learning skill? For example, a mnemonic to remember the colours of the rainbow or a song to help you remember the months of the year. Did you learn many more such techniques as you went through school? Do you use many of them today in different contexts?

Think of something you have learned in the past year which was challenging. What was it? Why did you learn it? How did you learn it? How might you have learned it better?

If someone asked you what kind of learner you are, what would you say? What if they asked you about the environment you prefer to learn in?

What were the three most useful things you learned at school? Who did you learn them from and how? Were they on the curriculum? How do you use those things today? What things do you wish you had learned at school but didn't? Did you learn about how you learn at school?

How much do you think your own views on and experiences of learning affect the way you work at school? Do your colleagues talk about their own learning? Do they talk about the learning of the pupils?

How would the pupils in your school describe the school? How would they describe learning? What would their responses be to the questions we asked over 2000 11-16-year-old pupils in the survey below?

Which three of the following do you do most often in class?

	2000 (%)	2002 (%)
Copy from the board or a book	56	63
Have a class discussion	37	31
Listen to a teacher talking for a long time	37	37
Take notes while my teacher talks	26	20
Work in small groups to solve a problem	25	22
Spend time thinking quietly on my own	22	24
Talk about my work with a teacher	22	16
Work on a computer	12	10
Learn things that relate to the real world	11	12

Source: MORI Omnibus Survey, 2000/2002

Since we cannot know what knowledge will be most needed in the future, it is senseless to try to teach it in advance. Instead, we should try to turn out people who love learning so much and learn so well that they will be able to learn whatever needs to be learned.

John Holt

For pupils ('learning to learn') has definitely changed their learning experience – a more positive atmosphere, an improved understanding of learning and it encourages them to be far more independent.

Teacher in 'learning to learn' project school

Overview

This chapter sets out why we believe teachers and senior managers in schools should consider developing a 'learning to learn' approach for their school. It provides a very brief overview of:

- what 'learning to learn' involves
- the research findings from Phase 2 of the project that indicate what 'learning to learn' can help teachers and schools achieve
- what developing an approach in their own school might mean in practice.

'Learning to learn': a new key skill?

What actually happens when we learn something? Does it differ for different people? Are some people better learners than others and how could the learning of everyone be improved?

'Learning to learn' is the search for answers to questions such as these and the ones on page 10. It is described in detail in Chapter 3 but, in brief, it offers learners an awareness of how they prefer to learn and their learning strengths; how they can motivate themselves and have the self-confidence to succeed; things they should consider, such as the importance of water, nutrition, sleep and a positive environment for learning; some of the specific strategies they can use, for example to improve their memory or make sense of complex information; and some of the habits they should develop, such as reflecting on their learning so as to improve next time.

In recent years knowing how to learn has come to be seen as the key skill required by employers in the twenty-first century. To paraphrase action learning guru Reg Revans, as everything changes around us we must learn at or faster than the rate of change to survive. People who know how to learn, and who can therefore adapt and change to new situations more effectively than those who must always be taken through new procedures step by step, will clearly be far more effective in a fast changing world.

Over the past two decades huge advances in technology and science have begun to reveal what actually happens when we learn, while cognitive psychology and other disciplines have begun to show how we can learn better. Most schools have not yet begun to engage with much of this new research and thinking. One thing that seems certain is that the old chalk-and-talk approach does not develop better learners. Peter Shrang was right when he said that the greatest distance in the world is that between what leaves the teacher's mouth and what enters the student's brain. Surprisingly, as the pupil responses to the MORI question on page 10 show, most classrooms have changed remarkably little since the days when their parents were at school.

From teaching to learning

'Learning to learn' gives you a renewed interest in teaching.

'Learning to learn' has transformed the way I teach and the way I think about teaching and learning.

Teachers in 'learning to learn' project schools

Why should heads, teachers or pupils be interested in how learning takes place, or how we could learn to learn better? Why not just focus on what is required by the National Curriculum or what is needed for the next test?

One good reason is the evidence for what 'learning to learn' can achieve from Phase 2 of the research, which is summarized in the boxes on pages 14 to 18 and set out in more detail in Chapter 5 of this book. In brief the research suggests that focusing on learning how to learn can help:

- raise standards of achievement

- raise teacher morale and motivation

- most importantly, make schools more effective, inclusive and motivating for a wider range of pupils.

Another reason is the testimony of the heads and teachers quoted throughout this book whose schools have been researching the impact of 'learning to learn' approaches over the past two years. Their view is that it is not enough for schools to be good at teaching, they must focus relentlessly on learning and on giving pupils the attitudes, skills and knowledge they need to carry on learning throughout life.

Creating a learning to learn school - research and practice for raising standards, motivation and morale

My priorities as a head are to enable the school to be in control of its teaching and learning environment; to promote a culture of professionalism and debate; to empower staff and children; to raise the self-esteem of pupils and to create learners who will take on the world (or feel they can).

Neil Baker, Headteacher, Christ Church Primary School, Wiltshire

Learning about learning is central to our school, not just learning stuff. The future is uncertain and what is needed is people who have confidence and belief in themselves as learners.

Steve Byatt, Headteacher, Ellowes Hall School, West Bromwich

The Phase 2 research project: headline findings

The research process is described in Chapter 4 and a more detailed version of these findings is included in Chapter 5. The full findings and related information (including an explanation of what data the schools collected and reported) are included in the Phase 2 Project Research Report available at www.campaign-for-learning.org.uk.

Research findings

The learner

There are positive effects on standards of achievement by pupils and the motivation of pupils, teachers and parents who understand and develop their preferred learning styles including VAK (Visual, Auditory, Kinesthetic), multiple intelligences and emotional intelligence, dominance profiles, learning dispositions and the 5 Rs for lifelong learning (Readiness, Resourcefulness, Resilence, Remembering, Reflectiveness).

❏ Students of all ages are more positive about learning and motivated to learn when they understand their preferred learning styles and intelligences.

❏ Encouraging the development of pupils' learning dispositions, including the 5 Rs for lifelong learning, enhances pupils' perceptions of themselves as learners and improves attainment levels.

❏ Pupils learn best when teachers present information in a range of ways to meet the different learning styles in their classrooms.

❏ Pupils learn best when they enjoy themselves or have fun, indicating that their emotional state is fundamental to learning.

Research findings

The learning process

There are positive effects on pupil standards, motivation and independence as learners where they understand models of brain-friendly, student-centred learning, including the importance of self-esteem and motivation in learning, and can identify and apply a range of strategies.

❏ Foundation Stage and Key Stage 1 and 2 pupils demonstrate increased enjoyment of and improved learning when they understand how they learn best and have a range of learning tools to apply to different tasks.

❏ 'Learning to learn' courses help primary and secondary students identify and apply a range of strategies that they think help them learn at school and at home.

❏ The vast majority of secondary students enjoy and value taking part in 'learning to learn' sessions and courses. They think 'learning to learn' courses are worthwhile, that what they learn helps with other school work and that they should be part of the regular school timetable.

❏ Parents who understand about 'learning to learn' approaches feel more confident about trying different ways to help their children learn at home.

Research findings

The learning environment

There are positive effects on standards and motivation of pupils associated with the location and physical environment of learning. Factors identified include the use of displays, pictures and music, the use of resources including ICT (Information and Communications Technology) and interactive whiteboards, and the consideration of pupil groupings in planning for learning.

❑ Attractive physical learning environments are associated with improved pupil attitudes, behaviour and performance.

❑ Posters, pictures and displays provide pupils with a structure through which to recognize, select and reinforce learning behaviours.

❑ The use of music as a tool for learning improves standards and motivation in secondary students.

Research findings

The teacher

Being involved in 'learning to learn' has enormous benefits for teacher motivation, ongoing CPD (Continuing Professional Development), their utilization of other adults in the classroom (for example, parents and teaching assistants) and for mentoring both pupils and colleagues.

❑ Improved pupil performance in examinations is associated with teachers who actively think about pedagogy.

❑ The vast majority of teachers found that both student learning and behaviour improved when they employed 'learning to learn' approaches.

❑ Teachers' professional motivation and enjoyment is increased when they adopt 'learning to learn' approaches.

❑ Active resistance by teachers and departments to 'learning to learn' correlates with pupil performance that is significantly below average.

❑ Parents who participate in a 'learning to learn' course become more effective in supporting their children's learning and report that they become better learners themselves.

❑ The roles of the headteacher and senior management in actively leading and supporting the development of 'learning to learn' approaches and a learning culture in the school are critical.

Research findings

The body

There are positive effects on standards and motivation of pupils related to hydration (that is, water available in classrooms), exercise and the use of relaxation techniques.

❏ Pupils learn better if they have free access to drinking water.

❏ Exercise in the forms of Brain Gym® and sport has a positive effect on pupil enjoyment of and motivation for learning.

❏ The use of music in classrooms has a positive effect on calming and relaxing pupils.

❏ Engaging in specific de-stressing activities before writing in examinations improves examination results.

But why 'learning to learn'?

'Learning to learn' has helped the pupils at our school to reflect on how they learn, and to begin to understand themselves as learners.

Quote from teacher in 'learning to learn' project school

Despite the reasons given in the last section, you may still feel that there are other ways to raise standards, that you are already motivated, or that you are simply too busy managing challenging behaviour, finding teachers to put in front of classes and preparing for Ofsted's visit next term to try something apparently non-essential like 'learning to learn'.

The answer to all these points is that of course 'learning to learn' is not the only way to raise standards, improve behaviour or achieve anything else in schools. You can achieve high standards without 'learning to learn', as Derek Wise, headteacher of Cramlington Community High School in Northumberland, implies:

'Learning to learn' approaches are not always the same as the approach needed for good exam results. You can succeed in exams through having a good memory and a teacher that chunks the work for you, pre-digests it so to speak. You can succeed in exams and not be a good learner.

Derek Wise, Headteacher, Cramlington Community High School, Northumberland

This is not to contradict the research finding above that 'learning to learn' can help raise standards, but it does recognize the complexity of the issues. A fascinating, but perhaps not altogether surprising finding from the project is that 'learning to learn' makes most difference (in terms of improved results and motivation) when it is taken up by teachers who are already achieving high standards and who are actively interested in pedagogy.

In the same way, despite the finding that 'learning to learn' can raise pupil motivation and self-esteem (thus helping improve behaviour), it will not ensure good behaviour on its own. Clearly, the approach must be built on firm foundations, with effective behaviour policies and sanctions in place if it is to work.

Making sense of initiative-overload for real school improvement

At the end of the day it is all about the quality of teacher–pupil interactions. If a teacher has respect for every pupil in their class and a belief in their ability to succeed, they won't misbehave. The little things are critical, like making sure there is a chair for every member of the class, greeting each one of them at the door and so on.

John Welham, AST, Camborne School, Cornwall

Ultimately, the real reason why schools should consider 'learning to learn' is suggested by John Welham's comment. To be interested in 'learning to learn' you must want more for your school and your pupils than just to get by and do the minimum required. It is potentially the most powerful approach any teacher can use to unleash the potential in his or her pupils. The simple truth is that the schools that have implemented 'learning to learn' over the past two years have done it because they have a passionate belief that learning should be central to their schools.

> *You can raise standards through a 'learning to learn' approach as well as you might through a more focussed exam-led approach, but with 'learning to learn' you have the bonus of a love of learning...A 'learning to learn' approach which permeates your school can do both.*

Derek Wise, Headteacher, Cramlington Community High School, Northumberland

> *There was a tendency in our school (before the project) for teachers to overteach and children to overlearn... I would say there is a culture of dependency in Hull and in our school, but 'learning to learn' is about overcoming that by developing independent learning whether in or out of the classroom.*

Sheila Ireland, Headteacher, Malet Lambert School, Hull

Another message that has come over consistently from the project school heads and teachers is that 'learning to learn' has enabled them to bring together the range of apparently disparate initiatives they are involved in and to make sense of these as part of a coherent philosophy and approach. In this way 'learning to learn' can help schools take control of their own agenda and destiny in the face of what can seem at times like bewildering externally driven change.

But the passion and commitment of these schools has paid off in very tangible ways as well. Back in September 2000 at the start of the project, the schools were at different stages. Some faced extremely challenging circumstances while others were successful but looking for a new challenge. Not all of the original 24 schools have continued as part of the project – seven dropped out because of staff changes or simply because the demands of completing a research project were too great given the other pressures on their time. Two others, when it came to it, simply did not have the time to write up the research they had done (see box on p. 96 for more details). But out of the schools that have remained involved:

- five are now specialist schools;
- three have received school improvement awards;
- most have received positive Ofsted reports for teaching and learning.

Equally, among the lead teachers on the project, one has been awarded an OBE, two have published books, many have been made ASTs (Advanced Skills Teachers) or Heads of Teaching and Learning within their schools, many more have completed Masters degrees or other qualifications and almost all are involved in giving INSET externally as part of regional or national networks.

> *Being involved in 'learning to learn' has transformed my career.*

Jackie Beere OBE, AST, Campion School, Northampton

West Grove Primary School

Enfield, London

Research area

'Learning to learn' strategies for Year 2 pupils

Hypothesis

'Learning to learn' strategies impact positively on pupil learning and achievement.

Research focus

Two cohorts of Year 2 pupils, a total of 84 pupils

Methodology

The ethos and strategies of 'learning to learn' have been embedded in teaching and learning throughout the school since it opened. This project used a computer programme that can predict KS1 national tests scores from Baseline Assessment data collected at the beginning of the Reception year. These data provide evidence of the effectiveness of 'learning to learn' for children's learning and achievement.

Comments from the recent Ofsted report regarding the school are reported.

Success criteria

Number of children who exceed their predicted score

Key findings

In the first cohort of 30 children,

- 60 per cent (N=18) exceeded their predicted score;
- 10 per cent (N=3) achieved at their predicted score;
- 23 per cent (N=7) did not have a predicted score because they were new to the school but all achieved at Level 2;
- 7 per cent (N=2) achieved at lower than their predicted score.

In the second cohort of 54 children,

- 54 per cent (N=29) exceeded their predicted score;
- 26 per cent (N=14) achieved at their predicted score;
- 6 per cent (N=3) did not have a predicted score because they were new to the school but all achieved at Level 2;
- 27 per cent (N=8) achieved at lower than their predicted score.

Rising trends in KS1 data:

Children achieving at Level 2 or above

	2001 (%)	2002 (%)
Reading	77	87
Writing	87	90
Maths	83	98

Children achieving at Level 3 or above

	2001 (%)	2002 (%)
Reading	10	30
Writing	10	14
Maths	10	33

Comments drawn from the Ofsted Report in 2001 included:

- 'a broad and interesting curriculum';
- 'pupils are very well motivated and show high levels of independence and willingness to learn';
- 'overall, the quality and range of learning opportunities are good';
- 'extra-curricular provision is good';
- 'the school is a socially inclusive school';
- 'the headteacher and her staff share a strong and appropriate vision of what they want to achieve and this is fully reflected in the work of the school'.

Conclusions

When 'learning to learn' teaching and learning strategies are embedded throughout the school, they impact positively on pupil learning and achievement.

So what does implementing a 'learning to learn' approach require from you?

The school thinks further than education and considers the whole child.

We do what we believe, not what we are told to do.

Teachers in 'learning to learn' project school

Chapter 6 outlines in more detail how you can develop a 'learning to learn' approach in your school. The key point to note here is that implementing 'learning to learn' does not necessarily require huge amounts of preparation time or significant budgets. It is certainly possible to take small first steps to find out more and to raise the profile among your colleagues.

This is not to suggest that developing 'learning to learn' is simple or something that can be delegated wholesale to an enthusiastic member of staff. 'Learning to learn' is not a set of study skills, some interesting facts about the brain or a bag of tricks you can teach your pupils so they become 'better' learners. 'Learning to learn' is more about an ethos that involves putting the learner at the centre by:

- schools providing the best possible learning environment, including linking with parents, employers and the wider community;

- teachers modelling learning and challenging pupils to develop their own learning wings; and

- pupils understanding themselves and their needs in a complex world and seeing practical ways to develop as lifelong learners.

As with any school-based initiative, this requires strong leadership from the head and Senior Management Team (SMT) of a school. Chapter 6 therefore includes specific advice drawn from the heads and SMTs of the project schools and wider sources to show how 'learning to learn' can be implemented.

That said, wherever you may currently be within a school you can begin to make changes to your own practice and thereby influence others. The question is what do you want to achieve and how does this fit with your other priorities? Whatever route you choose, we believe that the quest is the most important and exciting one that schools, teachers and learners can ever undertake. The goal is a school which can provide for the needs of all its pupils and help them understand themselves and how they learn so that they develop as motivated and effective learners able to make the most of their many talents throughout their lives.

The findings from the first two years of the 'learning to learn' project begin to provide a route map for this journey. We hope that this book will stimulate further debate and interest among an ever widening range of teachers and schools into how they can take the learning further. The Campaign for Learning is continuing to explore the how and why of 'learning to learn' along with a larger groups of schools as part of a larger three-year project.

Creating a learning to learn school - *research and practice for raising standards, motivation and morale*

2 | 'Learning to learn' in context: educational reform in a changing world

For young Britons in the twenty-first century teaching needs to serve three functions: the transmission of knowledge for a world built on information, the broadening of horizons in a country still scarred by disadvantage, and learning how to learn in preparation for a lifetime of change.

David Miliband MP, Minister of State for School Standards,
Northern Education Conference, January 2003

Outline

The 'learning to learn' project is focused on identifying the attitudes/attributes, skills and knowledge that people will need for life in the twenty-first century. We believe that people without these qualities and skills will struggle to succeed and become increasingly excluded as they fail to adapt in an ever-changing world. This chapter sets out:

- why 'learning to learn' is more important than ever in the twenty-first century;

- how the government's education reforms are working to develop a lifelong learning society; and

- areas where we believe policies could go further to develop a 'learning to learn' approach.

Life in the twenty-first century

For much of the last century it was considered perfectly normal to leave school at 16 and consider one's 'learning' to be over. The majority of men expected to go into blue-collar jobs that had changed little since their fathers' day, while the majority of women expected to stay at home and raise a family. Only two or three per cent of school leavers went to university.

Today, this picture seems a distant memory. In the workplace, 'jobs for life' have disappeared, women outnumber men, and new technologies are transforming the way we work.

These changes are inextricably linked to wider changes in the global economy. Faced by increased competition from countries where labour is cheap, the UK's economy has shifted from large scale manufacturing to high-tech industries, such as aerospace and pharmaceuticals, and value added services. Meanwhile, technological advances in computers and the internet have impacted enormously on traditional ways of working. Whereas, in the past, huge numbers of jobs did not require even basic literacy skills, today the vast majority involve intermediate or advanced skills.

Old industries (and many venerable British companies) have disappeared, while new ones are constantly emerging to undercut their established competitors and improve productivity. The nature of value has been transformed, even after the bursting of the dot.com bubble, and it is creative and inventive ideas quite as much as efficient delivery that matters in today's workplace.

Equally, the way we work has changed. Flexible working, home working, part-timers, job-shares, independent contractors: the options for employment have never been more varied, with the attendant danger that those without skills will fall through the cracks, without either employee rights or opportunities for training and development.

The flip-side of flexible working is networked workplaces, where technology allows for communication with people all over the world as easily as with our neighbour, putting a premium on communication skills. Relationships are the new bottom line.

So the need to keep up with international competition is relentless. But the UK's productivity rates are among the lowest in Europe, meaning that we have to work the longest hours just to remain competitive. We pride ourselves on our inventiveness and creativity, but need to invest far more in our learning if we are to capitalize on this and release the talents of all our people.

Learning to keep afloat

So today the UK's prosperity increasingly depends on the brains, not the brawn, of its citizens. We experience this in any number of different ways, from the regular need to update our computer skills, to the subtle shifts in organizational structure which have replaced hierarchies with self-managed teams and networks.

Meanwhile, we are faced by an array of social, ecological and political transformations that require sophisticated collective action. From global warming to the international 'war on terror'; from third world poverty to the spread of HIV; from gun crime to race riots; from the 'death of democracy' to increasing drug abuse: the potential issues threaten to overwhelm us as never before.

In our personal lives, we struggle to find meaning, balance and happiness. Family structures are becoming more fluid. We increasingly define ourselves according to a shifting set of identities that might include anything from our race, gender, sexuality or religious beliefs, to our shopping or television watching preferences.

Change is all around us and, while many people thrive in this fast-paced information packed environment, others struggle to keep up. The simple difference between those who sink and those who swim is learning. It is not coincidental that huge numbers of those in prison have poor basic skills or that those with university degrees earn exponentially more than the unqualified over the course of their lifetimes.

The evidence is clear: people with few skills are at ever greater risk of social and economic exclusion. We must learn not just to keep up, but to stay on top of life in the twenty-first century. But this is about far more than just individual success; the relentless individualism and consumerism of our media age requires thoughtful learning for both personal fulfilment and citizen engagement.

Education, education, education

The current government has recognized the scale of this challenge and made impressive moves to raise standards in schools, encourage more young people to stay on in education after the age of 16, and raise the skill levels of adults. A range of initiatives have been put in place to achieve the Department for Education and Skill's (DfES) over-arching aims.

Objective 1:   Give children an excellent start in education so that they have a better foundation for future learning.

Objective 2:   Enable all young people to develop and to equip themselves with the skills, knowledge and personal qualities needed for life and work.

Objective 3:   Encourage and enable adults to learn, improve their skills and enrich their lives.

These initiatives seemingly cover every aspect of education, from Sure Start programmes and enhanced early years provision, through to the newly merged National Literacy and Numeracy Strategies in primary schools, the Key Stage 3 strategy, Curriculum 2000 and Excellence in Cities to name a few. Most recently, the strategy document *14–19 opportunity and excellence* has set out plans for greater flexibility and choice in learning post-14, with less compulsory content beyond essential skills and a welcome attempt to bridge the traditional academic-vocational divide in education. The 2002 Education Act presaged further change, with schools given the option of radically innovating in all areas and a new Innovation Unit set up within the DfES in part to help this happen.

case
study

Kingdown School

Wiltshire, 11–18 Mixed Comprehensive

Research area

'Learning to learn' programmes for Year 9 pupils

Hypotheses

A learning community facilitates effective learning in Year 9.

The 'learning to learn' programme improves Year 9 pupils' confidence as learners.

Changes in the physical environment and school day help pupils learn.

Research focus

Current Year 9 pupils who have completed a three-year programme of 'learning to learn'

Methodology

The current Year 9 pupils completed a three-year programme of 'learning to learn' that included learning how to learn, multiple intelligences, preferred learning styles, how our brains work, thinking skills, study skills, mind mapping, target setting and speed reading.

A training day for teachers focused on improving the classroom environment was conducted at the start of the autumn term. Criteria for classrooms were agreed and 98 per cent of classrooms checked at the end of the day met the criteria.

The deputy head (Teaching and Learning) observed Year 9 lessons in all subject areas and provided feedback according to the agreed criteria.

Pupils in Year 9 completed a questionnaire at the end of term.

Success criteria

Improvements in Year 9 assessment tests results analysed against school targets and preferred modes of taking in information.

Key findings

1. Assessment test results compared to school targets at Level 5 or above

	Targets (%)	Results (%)
English	63	76
Maths	65	76
Science	57	76

Significant improvement in school targets (based on CATS scores) was achieved in the assessment test results. The English results were some of the best ever achieved at the school.

2. Percentage of pupils in each learning style who achieved Level 5 or above

	Visual (%)	Auditory (%)	Kinesthetic (%)
English	87	74	93
Maths	77	74	83
Science	78	64	87

The distribution of Year 9 pupils' preferred modes of taking in information was visual (38 per cent), auditory (17 per cent) and kinesthetic (45 per cent).

This data indicates that all learners are achieving success at Kingdown School and that the kinesthetic learners are slightly more successful. The data suggests that an appropriate range of teaching and learning styles is used in lessons.

Creating a learning to learn school - *research and practice for raising standards, motivation and morale*

3. Results from pupil questionnaires

Almost half of the pupils (49 per cent) reported feeling confident as a learner, although 43 per cent reported feeling unconfident and eight per cent were unsure about how confident they felt as a learner.

Over two-thirds of the pupils (76 per cent) thought that the organization of the school day helped them learn, with 19 per cent disagreeing and five per cent being unsure.

Over half of the pupils (56 per cent) thought that the classroom displays helped them with 43 per cent disagreeing.

4. Results from teaching observations

Lesson observations show that there is a high standard of teaching in Year 9 with staff using a variety of teaching and learning styles to engage all learners.

Conclusions

Although all learners were successful, the data suggests that 'learning to learn' approaches had an significant impact on approximately half of this Year 9 group.

Staff used a variety of teaching methods to engage all learners and a high standard of teaching in Year 9 was achieved.

The contributing factors to this success included:

■ hard work from the faculties

■ revision sessions after school and at weekends

■ the 'learning to learn' programme

■ mixed ability teaching in English

■ the focus on teaching and learning across the whole school

■ target setting across the school

■ seating plans

■ classroom environment.

Within the lifelong learning arena, we have seen the creation of the Learning and Skills Council with an £8bn budget to fund post-school learning outside Higher Education and with an express remit to drive up demand for learning and widen participation. Equally, initiatives such as Ufi/learndirect, the NHS university NHSU, and the adult basic skills strategy have received ongoing support and funding.

In the area of Higher Education, the target of 50 per cent of all young people to experience tertiary education before they are 30 is driving much of the agenda. The long-awaited White Paper *The Future of Higher Education* sets out how the government proposes to do this, predominantly through an expansion of work-focused Foundation Degrees. Universities will be given the right to raise additional funds through higher tuition fees subject to meeting requirements to widen participation, while it is hoped that the limited reintroduction of student grants and reforms to when and how student loans are repaid will entice greater number of working class and under-represented groups into universities.

Focusing on teaching and learning

Almost every single government education document includes some mention of high-quality teaching and learning, while many of them devote considerable resources to professional development.

In schools, huge emphasis is being put on supporting heads and senior managers through the new National College for School Leadership and the Leadership Incentive Grant. Equally, the creation of Advanced Skills Teachers, Advanced/Leading Edge Partnership Schools, and the National Grid for Learning/Curriculum Online, along with the massive investment in teachers' professional development through the national strategies, shows a welcome focus on high-quality teaching and learning. The simultaneous 'modernization of the teaching profession', for example through linking pay to performance and the expansion of Teaching Assistants and support staff represents a fundamental shift in the role and nature of teaching.

Some of these reforms have explicitly drawn on the thinking that has informed the 'learning to learn' project. Back in 1997 the then DfEE's *Excellence in Schools* White Paper stated that:

We want to see more examples of accelerated learning based on the latest understanding of how people learn (and of) the systematic teaching of thinking skills, which research has shown to be strongly associated with positive learning outcomes.

This statement has been backed up through action on a number of fronts, for example the inclusion of the Foundation Subjects strand in the Key Stage 3 strategy. This strand has proved highly popular with teachers and is heavily influenced by Thinking Skills, Assessment for Learning and other 'learning to learn' approaches.

The government's reform strategy

The reforms in schools are aimed at ensuring high standards for all and, increasingly, tailoring learning and broadening choice for individual pupils as they develop. Although they may sometimes appear chaotic and contradictory on the ground, the reforms have a clear strategic rationale originally set out by Professor Michael Barber when he was Head of the Standards and Effectiveness Unit at the DfES.

Writing in 2000 in the Campaign for Learning's collection of essays *Schools in the Learning Age,* Barber set out a blueprint for reform offering what he called 'high challenge, high support' to all professionals working in schools. Whereas previous administrations either had little ambition for the system or presented huge challenges but offered few resources or support to implement change, New Labour had adopted the following model:

Thus, challenging national targets for exam results, broken down to local level, drive the system, while performance tables and Ofsted results hold schools to account with both the government and parents. Schools are provided with both funds and high-quality support and are increasingly given more autonomy once they have proven their performance.

Looking to the future Barber wrote:

The school will remain crucial to providing the foundation of learning, the induction into democratic society and the constant support that every individual student needs, but it will cease to be the provider of all learning for each student. Instead, while it will provide some, it will also seek learning opportunities in other schools, in and out of school learning settings (such as museums), in the community, in the workplace or over the internet. It will be an advocate for the student and a guarantor of quality. Increasingly, teachers and heads will think not only outside the boundaries of their school building, but beyond their city and their country too. This process will truly represent the opening up of schools to the wider lifelong learning system that the twenty-first century will witness.

Tensions at the heart of the approach

The use of repeated practice tests impresses on pupils the importance of tests. It encourages them to adopt test taking strategies designed to avoid effort and responsibility. Repeated practice tests are, therefore, detrimental to high-order thinking.

Testing, motivation and learning, **Assessment Reform Group, 2002**

As schools are well aware, the government's approach has seen considerable success, with rising standards in most areas thanks to tremendous efforts by teachers. But, as the falling off of progress and the failure to reach the 2002 targets for Key Stage 2 literacy and numeracy suggest, there may be a limit to what this process of reform can achieve.

Michael Barber acknowledges in his *Schools in the Learning Age* article that one of the major sub-texts to these initiatives and improvements is the stress that they have put on teachers and schools. Certainly, the DfES is increasingly coming to recognize that teacher recruitment and retention is perhaps its greatest challenge and that failure to improve morale in the profession could scupper its efforts to raise standards. This has led to above inflation pay rises, golden handshakes and training salaries for new teachers as well as the review of workload and bureaucracy referred to above. However, despite some successes in increasing recruitment, major criticisms from existing teachers, who feel disempowered by centralized reforms and a lack of professional autonomy, have yet to be seriously addressed.

West Grove Primary School

Enfield London

Research area

The impact of 'learning to learn' on teachers and parents

Hypotheses

'Learning to learn' impacts positively on teacher morale.

'Learning to learn' impacts positively on parental perceptions of the school.

Research focus

Teaching and support staff

Parents

Methodology

Data were collected from:

- professional development interviews with all staff
- questionnaires to parents
- letters received from parents
- number of applications for posts advertised.

Success criteria

Positive attitudes from staff and parents

Increased numbers of applicants for posts advertised

Key findings

Qualitative comments from staff indicated that they find the embedding of 'learning to learn' in the school to be a positive experience for themselves, the children, teaching and learning.

- 'I've never been so inspired.'
- 'We feel like we are bouncing off the children all the time.'
- 'The school thinks further than education and considers the whole child.'

- 'I had heard of the West Grove way at my previous school and now I can see how well it works.'

- 'We do what we believe, not what we are told to do.'

- 'The empowerment and confidence given to staff and children, allowing us to be the best we can be.'

- 'We concentrate on learning rather than teaching.'

- 'The children learn better by being able to learn in the best way for them.'

Qualitative comments from parents reveal that they are very satisfied with the school's approach to teaching and learning for their children.

- 'Thank you for making West Grove what it is today and for making each child feel special.'

- 'Thank you for keeping S inspired and making West Grove a great place to be and learn.'

- 'The West Grove way recognizes and makes use of children's interests and strengths and uses them to help them learn.'

With a return rate of 56 per cent, data from parent questionnaires indicated that:

- 98 per cent of parents reported that their child liked school.

- 95 per cent thought that their child was making good progress at school.

- 88 per cent thought they were well informed about how well their child was getting on.

- 86 per cent thought that the school expects their child to work hard to achieve their best.

- 95 per cent thought that the school was helping their child become mature and responsible.

- 82 per cent thought that the school provides an interesting range of activities outside lessons.

Data regarding applications for advertised posts indicated that advertisements for five teaching posts attracted over 30 applications and those for four support staff posts resulted in over 48 application packs being sent out in the first week.

Conclusions

When 'learning to learn' teaching and learning strategies are embedded throughout the school, they impact positively on the attitudes and perceptions of the school among teachers, support staff, parents and prospective employees. A high degree of satisfaction with the school's approach to teaching and learning for primary children was expressed by teachers, support staff and parents.

Another key question is whether the government's reforms will support those most at risk of social exclusion to fulfil their potential. There is no doubt that the government is committed to this, and reforms such as Sure Start, Excellence in Cities and the ConneXions service are specifically aimed at meeting this objective. But, while 80 per cent of young people from Social Class 1 professional families enter higher education today, just 14 per cent of those from Social Class 5 do. Greater support is clearly needed. Perhaps we will also need to test out more imaginative approaches to defining a curriculum for all.

Most fundamental of all is the question of whether Barber's twin system of accountability and autonomy is workable, or whether the need for accountability measured through test results will always stifle true learning. Critiques of the rigidity and overemphasis on skills training in the National Literacy Strategy are an example of this. Researchers have found numerous examples of teachers 'teaching to the test' and spending inordinate amounts of classroom time drilling pupils using centrally prepared lesson-plans with little creative input or differentiation. Meanwhile, pupils learn ever more firmly that achievement in learning equals achievement in the tests, and not surprisingly parents become increasingly concerned at the levels of stress placed on their children.

The evidence from the 'learning to learn' project summarized in Chapter 5 corroborates numerous other studies which have shown that it is the quality of teacher–pupil interaction and dialogue that defines deeper learning and the development of learning dispositions. To simplify the debate: what is the value of even 100 per cent achievement in national test results if all those children do not grow up wanting to use their literacy skills and learn more? While the introduction of value added performance tables and the emphasis on school autonomy are welcome, the government must revisit its strategy for educational reform if it is truly to create a Learning Age.

Towards the school of the future?

We have got to do a lot fewer things in school. The greatest enemy of understanding is coverage. As long as you are determined to cover everything you actually ensure that most kids are not going to understand. You have got to take enough time to get kids involved in something so they can think about it in lots of different ways and apply it – not just in school but at home and on the street and so on.

Professor Howard Gardner, Harvard University

It would be wrong to suggest that the government is not thinking about the future of schooling and learning. Much of its thinking and investment has been in the role technology could play in supporting future learning, with pilots underway to explore what the Classroom of the Future would look like and the Curriculum Online initiative already underway. *Transforming the way we learn*, the DfES's publication setting out its thinking on this, is welcome in its recognition that no amount of technology will reduce the need for teachers to facilitate effective learning.

But as Professor Howard Gardner indicates in the above quote, the danger is always that yet another new requirement will be added to the already bulging curriculum, meaning that teachers will continue to have to cover the curriculum content and summative assessment will remain the key focus of pupils' learning. If this is the case, then standards will mean little beyond the ability of both sides to play the learning game.

This is not to say that the government is not aware of the need for education to develop a broader set of skills and attitudes than those assessed by national tests and GCSEs. This can be seen in support for out-of-school hours learning, the new citizenship curriculum, learning mentors and extended schooling approaches, to name just a few.

Equally, the 14–19 reforms will reduce the statutory curriculum from Key Stage 4. One of the key aims of the reforms is to increase motivation and achievement so that more young people continue learning through to 19 and beyond. This is welcome, as is the genuine attempt to strengthen the vocational route and increase its parity with the traditional academic one.

But there are limitations in the extent to which changes to the 14–19 curriculum and qualifications framework will genuinely motivate many young people who are currently switched off by schooling. It remains to be seen whether the more radical proposal in the original green paper that students would be able to choose where they learn for significant amounts of time, either in school, college or the workplace, will actually be followed through. The 14–19 paper is also unclear on the strategy for engaging the nine per cent of young people identified in Bridging the Gap as not in education, training or employment or for ensuring that the 15 per cent of young people in work but not receiving formal learning get their chance.

The emphasis on teachers' professional development and opening up the curriculum to give pupils greater choice over where and what they learn is welcome. Ultimately, however, the questions asked of all these reforms must be whether in schools of the future pupils will answer the question MORI asked them (see page 10) differently and whether surveys of adult attitudes to and participation in learning begin to show a shift in the future.

What about 'learning, learning, learning'?

The brain (is) a non-linear, self-organizing system…The integration of constructivist learning theory, knowledge of learning styles and knowledge of brain physiology create an emergent set of practices that look much more like what we might design if we set out to create a brain compatible learning environment poised 'on the edge of chaos': open enquiry-based constructivist learning; co-operative learning; integrated theoretic instruction; authentic assessment; and community-based learning.

John Cleveland, The Chaos Network, 1994

Good teachers have always known how to motivate pupils, present information in a variety of engaging ways and ensure that real learning takes place in the classroom. But, equally, the narrow focus of most initial teacher training and ongoing support for teachers, coupled with the huge pressures on them to maintain discipline, cover the curriculum and achieve results prevents many others from doing so. Currently, in the drive to raise standards, pupils must sit as passengers and learning takes a back seat.

Simply working harder to raise standards along the same lines will only produce ever more teacher overload and burn-out. One cannot help but feel that there is only limited further improvement to be achieved from the rather weary old nag that is the school system as we know it today.

What is needed is a clear unifying vision of what learning is, what it is for, and how it is best done at the heart of our education strategy. The question it must answer is: How can our education system actually motivate and equip young people for life in the twenty-first century? As John Cleveland implies in the quote at the start of this section, this might require some radical thinking about how and where learning takes place.

It is remarkable how little this question is asked of the activity in today's schools. While debates rage about 'A' level marking or whether Shakespeare should be compulsory in the National Curriculum, serious analysis of the dispositions and skills possessed by successful lifelong learners and the ways in which these might best be developed by schools has only just begun to reach the agenda.

What is needed, as the Campaign for Learning has already suggested, is a national strategy for learning that encompasses the full range of learning for the full range of life – from cradle to grave. Within this strategy:

- funding structures would be reviewed to recognize that it is in the early years that we need the richest and most supportive learning environment possible in order to develop positive dispositions for learning;

- school improvement would be determined according to factors such as engagement with the community, parental involvement, staff morale and an emphasis on teaching and learning, quite as much as raising achievement in terms of grades;

- the curriculum and assessment system would be focused on developing basic skills (the 'old' three Rs) and the 5 Rs for lifelong learning outlined in the next chapter, and would be fit for purpose so that assessment complemented rather than defined the learning process; and

- pupils would be immersed in a range of real-world learning activities and would be guided in taking responsibility for their own learning.

In setting up the 'learning to learn' project, our hypothesis has been that if such an approach could show a way of developing these skills and the teaching approaches required to support them, while simultaneously raising standards and the motivation of both groups, it might also help to inject some joy back into teaching. The reaction of the teachers involved shows that we were right.

Creating a learning to learn school - *research and practice for raising standards, motivation and morale*

3 What is 'learning to learn'? The thinking behind the project

I decided to be part of this national action research project because I am concerned that we are not applying what we already know about the brain and how we learn most effectively. I am deeply impressed by the calibre of thinking being brought to the project's development and convinced that, through reflective practice and with support from academic researchers, we can begin to establish what works and why.

Michael Wood, Headteacher, Cornwallis School, Kent

We don't unpack the learning process sufficiently. Children see Wordsworth's final draft and think that he turned it out fully formed, so he's a genius and they're not.

Derek Wise, Headteacher, Cramlington Community High School, Northumberland

Overview

This chapter sets out the thinking behind the project and what we actually mean by 'learning to learn'. It covers:

- the definition of 'learning to learn' and the key areas that the project schools investigated;

- what the project has come to see as the essential attitudes/attributes, skills and knowledge of an effective lifelong learner, described within the 5 Rs model;

- what each of the 5 Rs actually involve and practical approaches schools can use to develop each one; and

- summaries of some of the main approaches that the project schools have used.

Before you start this section...

Try this short activity, ideally with someone else.

- A man and a woman are standing side by side each with his or her weight on his or her right foot.
- They begin by walking so that each steps out on his or her left foot.
- The woman takes three steps for each two steps of the man.
- How many steps does the man take before his right foot strikes the ground at the same time as the woman's right foot?

Use this box if it helps you think:

When you have finished, think about how you solved the problem.

- By walking along side by side with your partner?
- By drawing the steps in the box?
- By 'walking' your fingers along the table?
- By working out the ratio in your head?

(From *The Mindgym*)[1]

The elements of 'learning to learn'

Before you start reading this chapter, work out the answer to the puzzle above, ideally with a colleague. The important thing is not the answer, but how you worked it out. If you did it with a group of people you would see different pairs using different approaches.

The point of the activity is simply to make clear that we all learn in different ways. It is widely accepted that all learners are born with a starter kit of reflexes, rudimentary maps and crude sets of responses. Neurological research evidence from Susan Greenfield and others indicates that the brain is programmed to tune itself in response to experience. Thus, every learner is unique in the way his or her brain has tuned itself in response to his or her own experience.

---

[1] The answer is that the man takes four steps, by which time the women has taken six.

Critically, in direct contrast to the first definition of intelligence as something innate and fixed in the box below, it appears that the natural learning ability of the brain can either be augmented or diminished as a result of the learners' experience. As a result of this, we each develop preferred ways of doing things and so what works for one person may not work for someone else. More importantly, simply stretching our learning muscles makes them stronger. Thus we can not only learn better learning skills, we can actually become better learners.

These observations have influenced the Campaign's definition of 'learning to learn' as:

'a process of discovery about learning. It involves a set of principles and skills which, if understood and used, help learners learn more effectively and so become learners for life. At its heart is the belief that learning is learnable.'

Thus 'learning to learn' is about understanding the process of learning and about developing strategies for improving our own learning. What the definitions intelligence, thinking, learning and metacognition in the boxes below suggest is that this is by no means an uncontested field. If our definition of intelligence can vary so dramatically over time, is there any point in learning how to learn when the thinking may change in the future? The answer is that there is no right way of 'learning to learn', in many ways it is the opening up of different avenues that stimulates an interest and awareness of possibility within pupils and adults.

Some definitions

Intelligence

The chief determiner of human conduct is a unitary mental process which we call intelligence... this process is conditioned by a nervous mechanism which is inborn...(and) is but little adapted by any later influence.

H.H. Goddard, 1920, quoted in *The Mismeasure of Man* (Revised Edition), Gould S (Penguin Books Ltd, 1995)

What you use when you don't know what to do.

Piaget

Multiple – verbal, mathematical-logical, spatial, musical, personal, interpersonal, intrapersonal, kinesthetic, naturalist.

Gardner

Thinking

High quality thinking – difficult to define but easy to recognize!

- Is not routine – the path of action is not usually known in advance.
- Tends to be complex – the total path is not 'visible' from a single viewpoint.
- Yields multiple rather than unique solutions.
- Involves nuanced judgement and interpretation.
- Can involve the application of multiple criteria which may conflict with one another.
- Involves uncertainty – not everything about the task at hand is known.
- Involves imposing meaning – finding structure in apparent disorder.
- Is effortful – considerable mental work is needed for the kinds of elaborations and judgements required.

Resnick (1987)

Learning

Learning is a consequence of thinking.

D. Perkins, *Smart Schools*, The Free Press, 1992

Learning is a process of active engagement with experience that may involve an increase in skills, knowledge, understanding, a deepening of values or the capacity to reflect. Effective learning leads to change, development and desire to learn more.

Campaign for Learning definition

Learning is a process of knowledge construction, not simply knowledge recording or absorption. This we know as Constructivism. Learning is knowledge dependent, with learners using current knowledge to construct new knowledge. Yet context matters greatly. The constructivist brain is a self-organizing system that is progressively shaped by its interaction with objects and events in the world around. We actually build the structures of our brains as we use them.

John Abbot, Learning…Seeing the Big Picture, unpublished

Metacognition

Metacognition: the ability to think about thinking, to be consciously aware of oneself as a problem solver, and to monitor and control one's mental processing.

John Bruer

So what does 'learning to learn' actually involve?

This section summarizes how the thinking behind the project evolved. When we started out on the 'learning to learn' project early in 2000, we created the mind map on the next page as way of showing visually what we saw as its key elements. At the end of the first year, we worked with teachers from the project schools to refine it in the light of the first year's experience and this led to the mind map on page 45. You can see on that map which schools were researching which area in Phase 2.

These maps only give a snapshot of our thinking about the elements involved in 'learning to learn', and already this has moved on. Certainly, if we were redrawing the maps today, we would want to include a much clearer indication that how you feel – the emotional/affective side of learning – is hugely important, and to recognize the excellent work being done on Thinking Skills and Assessment for Learning more clearly. This is an important point to note, since it would be completely wrong to suggest that the project has found the 'answers' to how we learn or can learn to learn.

As always with a relatively new area which has not yet become part of the culture, one of the difficulties is in finding an accessible but precise language to express concepts. Achieving this is essential if learners and teachers are to be able to talk about learning in the same way that they might use technical terms such as 'metaphor' to talk about a poem or a story. To help in this, and to avoid unnecessary detail in the main text, we have included boxed summaries explaining some of the key areas of thinking and practice used in describing 'learning to learn' throughout this section.

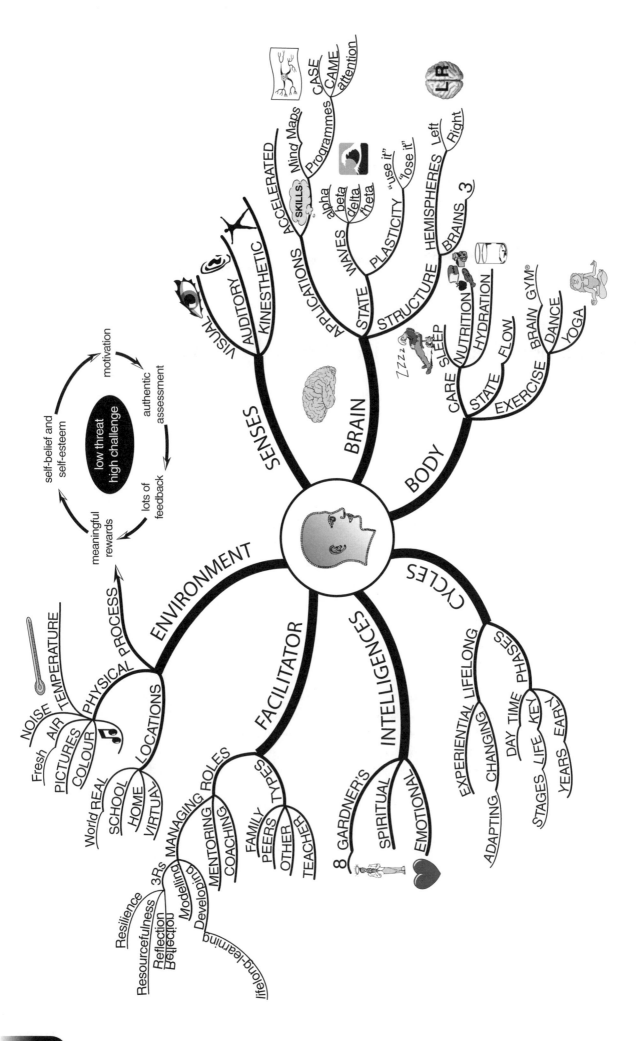

Mind map showing the elements of 'learning to learn' used in Phase 1

Creating a learning to learn school - *research and practice for raising standards, motivation and morale*

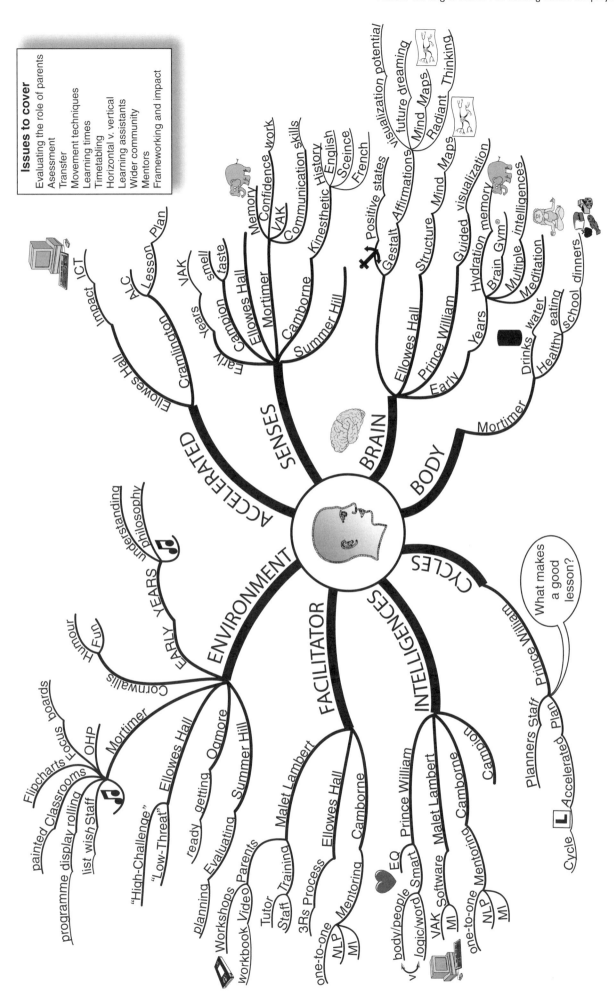

Issues to cover

Evaluating the role of parents
Asessment
Transfer
Movement techniques
Learning times
Timetabling
Horizontal v. vertical
Learning assistants
Wider community
Mentors
Frameworking and impact

Mind map showing the elements of 'learning to learn' used in Phase 2

The thinkers and projects that have influenced 'learning to learn'

The research tells us that successful learning occurs when learners have ownership of their learning; when they understand the goals they are aiming for; when, crucially, they are motivated and have the skills to achieve success. Not only are these essential features of effective day to day learning in the classroom. They are key ingredients of successful lifelong learning.

Assessment for Learning: beyond the black box, Assessment Reform Group, 1999

What the mind maps show is that the project has drawn on, and is indebted to, a wealth of thinking and practice from a range of different disciplines. The theory and research sources underpinning 'learning to learn' include cognitive psychology, neuroscience, theories of learning and intelligence, work on formative assessment and thinking skills, motivational psychology, emotional intelligence, learning environments, health and nutrition.

The list of initiatives on page 119 and the resources section at the back of this book begin to show the range of thinkers and practical initiatives on the ground and the range of thinkers that have influenced the project and the schools over the course of the two years. These different influences and disciplines have different degrees of theoretical and research grounding. Some have emerged from academic research, others from teachers in schools simply going with 'what works' or what feels right. One of the aims of the project has always been to bring together these different aspects and perspectives and to establish a consensual set of theories and practices backed by robust research-based evidence for their effectiveness. The Campaign will continue to do this in Phase 3 of the research.

What makes a good lifelong learner?
The goal for 'learning to learn'

The following section sets these different theories and approaches into a single model for 'learning to learn', defined as the 5 Rs for lifelong learning, which has influenced the thinking and practice of many of the schools in Phase 2 and will form the basis for the research in Phase 3.

The 5 Rs model seeks to define what the end goal of a 'learning to learn' approach in a school should be. What actually makes a good lifelong learner? Or, what would an effective 'learn to learner' know and do?

The first point to note is that effective lifelong learners seem to have, first and foremost, positive attitudes, attributes or dispositions. Think of the example of literacy and reading as an analogy for learning. We know that having the skill of literacy does not necessarily mean that we choose to read. A much more subtle range of factors influence whether people see themselves as readers and are motivated to pick up a book. Similarly, a good lifelong learner requires positive attitudes in addition to a range of skills and a considerable amount of knowledge.

These dispositions are influenced by a whole range of factors, many of them outside the school's immediate control. We are all born curious, but the socializing culture of home, peers and school that children grow up in somehow turns many of them off learning. Unnourished by success, challenge and practice their appetite for learning can wither. Although, of course, they will continue to learn, they may not see themselves as learners and will certainly not develop the dispositions and skills of the most effective learners.

The new 5 Rs for lifelong learning

Professor Guy Claxton, a member of the project's Advisory Board, has suggested that in addition to the old three Rs of Reading, wRiting and aRithmetic, the new three Rs for lifelong learning should be Resilience, Resourcefulness and Reflectiveness. More recently he has added Reciprocity as a fourth R. Another Advisory Board member, Alistair Smith, has developed this thinking with the suggestion that there should be 5 Rs (Resilience, Resourcefulness, Responsibility, Reasoning and Reflectivity) and has begun work with several LEAs to assess how these can be developed.

The 'learning to learn' project has taken Claxton's original three and added two additional ones: Readiness and Remembering. The attitudes/attributes, skills and knowledge that we see making up these new five Rs are outlined in the chart on pages 48 and 49. Many of the schools in Phase 2 of the project looked at how they could develop these dispositions, and the findings are given in Chapter 5. One of the project schools, Christ Church Primary, has also been involved in the ELLI project which is looking at the same issues (see box on pages 82 and 83).

In the following sections, the key elements of each of the 5 Rs are outlined in more detail.

The new 5 Rs of the effective Learn to Learner

Attitudes/Attributes	Skills - Demonstrates ability to:	Knowledge - Knows how:
Readiness		
• Motivation • Curiosity • Self-belief/esteem • Self-efficacy (optimism re the learning outcome, confidence and willingness to take risks)	• Assess and manage own motivation • Achieve a positive learning state • Manage own learning process	• To assess own motivation • To set goals and connect to the learning • To achieve a positive learning state, including your preferred learning environment
Resourcefulness		
• Learning from and with others • Learning creatively in different ways • Flexibility	• Make most of preferred learning style • Develop and expand learning repertoire and to harness creativity • Find and use information • Communicate effectively in different ways (including pacing, VAK, etc.)	• The mind works and how humans learn • To assess own preferred learning style and environment • To use different approaches to learning • To seek out and use information, including through ICT • To communicate effectively in different ways (including pacing, VAK, etc.)
Resilience		
• Keeping going • Learning under stress • Managing feelings about learning and teachers, peers and resources	• Persistence and managing optimism and self-belief • Empathize and use EQ • Use different approaches when stuck	• To apply learned optimism and self-efficacy approaches • To empathize and use EQ approaches • To procede when stuck • To ask (critical) questions

Attitudes/Attributes	Skills - Demonstrates ability to:	Knowledge - Knows how:
Remembering		
● Maximizing your memory ● Applying learning ● Practising	● Different memory approaches ● Make connections ● Apply learning, including in different contexts (transfer)	● To use different memory approaches ● To make connections ● To apply learning, including in different contexts
Reflectiveness		
● Looking back ● Improving learning and performance	● Stop, reflect (e.g. ask questions, observe, see patterns), experiment and evaluate learning	● To ask questions, observe, see patterns), to experiment and to evaluate learning

1. Readiness

At its simplest, Readiness is about the factors that need to be in place before learning begins so that learners are effectively primed and ready to learn. The key elements of this can be summarized as:

- managing your own learning process

- motivation

- curiosity

- self-belief/esteem and

- self-efficacy.

This section gives a detailed outline of some of the different models of learning that can help learners manage their learning effectively. It finishes by listing some of the other relatively simple approaches schools can adopt to develop areas such as self-esteem, motivation, goal setting and achieving a positive learning state.

Managing your learning

There is plenty of evidence that you cannot learn if you are not emotionally and psychologically ready for it. Put crudely, you cannot learn on an empty stomach or with your self-esteem in tatters. But even if these factors are in place, you still need to be motivated to learn effectively. Indeed, even in apparently smoothly run classes, many pupils may be playing intellectual truant if they have not been engaged. We believe that an effective learner would have a sense of how they could try to influence these factors. Furthermore, they would have a language to describe their learning and a meta-cognitive awareness of how they were doing it. This awareness might involve:

- being clear about why they were learning something (having a goal/seeing the relevance) and

- being clear about how they would learn it (asking for the Big Picture/choosing their optimal learning environment/having a route map or model of how the learning might take place).

Models of learning

What motivated me most was the thought that if I do a good piece of work, it will be displayed around the school.

We were working towards something at the end of it – we did it all ourselves.

Quotes from 'learning to learn' project school Year 9 pupils

Learning is a process, although often a messy one. One of the essential elements of Readiness is therefore having a model of learning, a route map that can guide you and help you think about the learning process you are undertaking. This is essential for learners to be able to manage their own learning process. There are many different models of learning and each one is appropriate for different learners and in different contexts. This section outlines some of the models either commonly in use or that have particularly influenced the project.

In *Learning to learn: setting the agenda for schools in the 21st century*, the publication which initially set out the 'learning to learn' project, we presented the following model of learning:

- being ready to learn
- being able to set and achieve goals
- knowing how to learn best
- harnessing creativity
- being able to reflect, adapt and change.

Building on this model, in *Teaching pupils how to learn* we developed a simpler Ready, Go, Steady model identifying three main stages to learning: 'before', 'during' and 'after'. These three stages are set out opposite, with the kinds of questions that each one raises for learners indicated.

Ready	**Before:** Being ready to learn Being able to set and achieve goals	How can we manage our emotional state so that we are ready to learn? How much self-esteem do we need to have? Do we need to connect ourselves to and engage fully in the learning we are being offered? What do we need to know about motivation and how to motivate ourselves to learn? What kinds of intrinsic and extrinsic rewards work? How do we reduce our learning to manageable chunks?
Go	**During:** Knowing how to learn best Harnessing creativity	How many different strategies do we have? Do we have the capacity to keep on learning when things get tough? What do we know about our own preferred learning styles and about how we like to take in data? Do we understand how our memory works? Do we have a model of a typical learning cycle? Are we in touch with our feelings? How do we use electronic media? Can we tolerate reasonable amounts of confusion, frustration and even uncertainty in our learning? Do we know how to ask questions and when to seek help? Do we assume that we have many intelligences? Are we able to listen to our hunches? Do we have strategies for thinking different thoughts and solving difficult problems?
Steady	**After:** Being able to reflect, adapt and change	How do we know how we are progressing? What is our attitude to making mistakes? Do we do things differently as a result of what we have learned? Do we know how to give and receive feedback? How well do we recognize what we have learned informally?

An underlying assumption of this model, and hence the deliberate move away from the natural order of Ready, Steady, Go, is that we need to focus more on the before and after, rather than on the middle bit.

A third model that many teachers will know is the Accelerated Learning Cycle developed by Alistair Smith, which is reproduced on the following page. This model was taken by one of the 'learning to learn' project schools, Cramlington Community High School in Northumberland, and developed as a framework for all lesson planning, thus ensuring that all teachers consider how they are meeting learners' needs throughout their lessons. Cramlington's innovative work on this and other areas of 'learning to learn' is explained more fully in *Creating an Accelerated Learning School* (see Resources section at end of book), which includes practical tools and techniques.

What is 'accelerated learning'?

CREATE THE SUPPORTIVE
LEARNING ENVIRONMENT
CONNECT THE LEARNING
BIG PICTURE FIRST
DESCRIBE THE OUTCOMES
INPUT
ACTIVITY
DEMONSTRATE
REVIEW FOR RECALL & RETENTION

From *Accelerated Learning in Practice*, p. 24, Network Educational Press Ltd, 1999

'Accelerated learning' is widely used in workplaces to provide high impact training and is increasingly well known in schools. The following description is taken from the work of Alistair Smith, one of accelerated learning's most well known thinkers and proponents in schools.

First and throughout, we create and sustain a positive,
supportive and challenging learning environment.

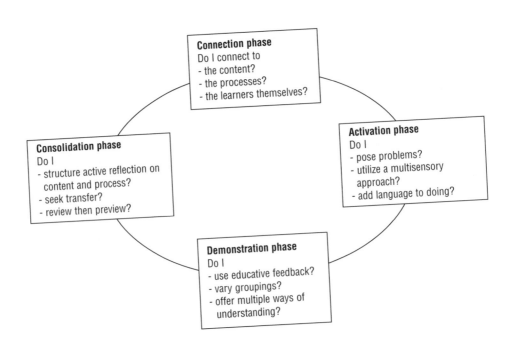

Connection phase
Do I connect to
- the content?
- the processes?
- the learners themselves?

Activation phase
Do I
- pose problems?
- utilize a multisensory approach?
- add language to doing?

Demonstration phase
Do I
- use educative feedback?
- vary groupings?
- offer multiple ways of understanding?

Consolidation phase
Do I
- structure active reflection on content and process?
- seek transfer?
- review then preview?

Learning is 'activated' when a learner makes a personal commitment to engage with learning. This involves risk. You help learners overcome perceived risk throughout the *connections phase*. As you do so, help learners connect both to the academic content and to the learning processes. As a teacher you also connect to learners as individuals and encourage them, in turn, to connect to each other as a community of learners.

In the *activation phase* you scaffold challenge by posing problems and seeking solutions. You also provide the relevant contextual data for this process to take place. You give necessary information. Where possible, and appropriate, use a multisensory approach: remember there are no memorable worksheets! Encourage learners to experience through seeing, hearing and doing. Encourage purposeful language exchange about process and content.

In the *demonstration phase* learners use multiple modes to 'show they know'. Gardner's model of multiple intelligence provides a useful frame for this. This is not a terminus: the demonstration phase is an opportunity for several rehearsals, for exchange of process and content understanding in a variety of groupings. It is also an opportunity for you to provide educative feedback. Educative feedback is specific advice about process and content improvement which can be acted on there and then. The *demonstration phase* takes most of our shared time.

In the *consolidation phase* learners reflect on what they have learned and how they have learned it. They do this in any combination of paired, small group or whole-class activity. Reflection links to the process and content outcomes which were shared in the connections phase. You begin to look at how the new learning may be transferred to different contexts. In advance of your next shared learning experience, you signal what is to come next time around.

All meaningful learning involves risk – teachers help learners negotiate the risk.

Alistair Smith's cycle is particularly useful for teachers planning more conscious learning, while the well known model describing the move from unconscious incompetence to conscious competence in the illustration below works well for less formal and experiential learning, such as learning to drive a car.

This model is also a useful one to bear in mind when thinking about 'learning to learn'. Achieving unconscious competence in 'learning to learn', so that we inhabit its ways of working throughout our lives with only occasional conscious monitoring and tweaking, must be the desired aim. While we are suggesting that for too long pupils have been expected to somehow absorb the skills involved in learning by osmosis and that therefore schools should teach and model them more explicitly, we are not suggesting that every adult should be forever consciously monitoring their learning.

case study

Prince William School

Northamptonshire, 13–18 Mixed Comprehensive Upper

Research area

Brain Gym® or Educational Kinesiology

Hypothesis

Using Brain Gym® in a systematic and structured way enhances performance and motivation in subjects for which Year 9 pupils experience difficulty.

Research focus

Year 9 pupils in the bottom sets of mathematics

Methodology

A target group was matched with an equivalent bottom set comparison group taking Year 9 mathematics. The comparison group was taught in the traditional way. The target group was taught by a maths teacher who was trained in Brain Gym®. The target group began each lesson with P.A.C.E., a four-stage introductory set of techniques that involved water drinking and body movements.

Success criteria

Improved assessment tests results

Increased enjoyment of the subject

Positive attitudes to learning

Key findings

The Year 9 target group's assessment tests results in 2002 were compared with those of the comparison group. Seven of the target group achieved a Level 5 compared with one in the comparison group.

The pupils in the target group reported enjoying maths more than those in the comparison group and reported Brain Gym® as a significant factor in their enjoyment. Overall, the target group reported more positive, motivated attitudes and enhanced assessment tests results.

There is growing awareness across the school of the value of Brain Gym® with pupils drinking more water, bringing water bottles to examinations and using specific de-stressing exercises before writing in examinations to good effect.

Conclusions

There is clear evidence that the majority of students improved their attitude and their performance in mathematics where Brain Gym® was used systematically.

Of course, there are many other models of learning, such as Vygotsky's zones of proximal development, Bloom's taxonomy and Kolb's learning cycle. With so many valuable models available, we are not prescribing any particular one. The point is that Readiness for learning requires that both teachers and pupils have a model which they can use as a scaffold for thinking about where they are in their learning, what strategies they can use to maximize that learning and where they are going next. Imagine if every time a pupil learned a new concept he or she thought – 'right, now where and how can I apply that to make sure I internalize and remember it?'

Other Readiness approaches

If you could sum 'learning to learn' up in one word, for me, it is self-belief and for the children as well.

It's giving the children encouragement and self-belief.

Parents of 'learning to learn' project school children

So what else can schools and teachers do to develop Readiness in their pupils?

Pupil self-esteem and dealing with issues outside school	<ul><li>A simple NLP technique is simply to ask pupils to roll up anything that has been bothering them into an imaginary ball of paper and put it in the bin at the start of each class (see box on page 62).</li><li>Circle time offers a more systematic approach to developing self-esteem and emotional intelligence by teaching and modelling certain learning 'rules' and allowing pupils to talk about wider issues in a safe and supportive environment (see box on pages 67 and 68).</li><li>Several of the 'learning to learn' project schools ran lessons where pupils 'searched for the hero inside them' – i.e. identified and celebrated their learning strengths.</li></ul>
Knowing how to assess your motivation, set goals and connect to the learning	<ul><li>A simple definition of motivation is that it depends on the learner seeing value in the learning (i.e. that it will help them achieve a valued goal) and believing that they will succeed in the learning and thereby achieve the hoped for outcome.</li><li>Motivation therefore rests on pupils feeling confident they can achieve, which relates to self-esteem (see above), and having challenging but achievable learning goals.</li><li>Research shows that giving rewards or unconditional praise does not necessarily help motivation. Assessment for Learning approaches (see box on pages 65 and 66) involving formative feedback on progress and areas for development are more effective.</li><li>In developing this aspect of Readiness, it is important to remember that children and adults have very different personas in different contexts. The teenager who is monosyllabic in class may become animated when given the chance to build a robot at home or to mess around on a computer. Connecting to the learning requires a broad definition of what learning is and where it takes place and finding ways to tap into pupils' practical life experience.</li></ul>

	● Starter activities that involve brainstorming prior knowledge and setting the Big Picture purpose of the learning are effective for connecting.
Knowing how to achieve a positive learning state, including your preferred learning environment	● Breakfast clubs offer an excellent way of ensuring that pupils aren't too hungry to learn. Equally, pupils and parents will benefit from practical advice on the importance of diet, sleep, water in class. ● Research on learning environments shows that they need to be personalized (e.g. by using display), active (e.g. through including participative, independent and investigative learning activities) and differentiated so that all learners can achieve. The use of colour, light and facilities that are fit for learning will also be essential. As always with 'learning to learn' the important factors should be made explicit so that pupils can identify and influence their own preferred environment.

2. Resourcefulness

Children learn better by being able to learn in the way that is best for them.

Teacher in 'learning to learn' project school

Resourcefulness is essentially about understanding how you personally learn and having a range of practical tools you can use to enhance your learning. It also includes the important skill of communication, in all its forms, since this is so essential to life and learning. The key elements of Resourcefulness can be described as:

● understanding your own preferred learning style, including how to take in information;

● understanding different approaches to learning, including how to harness your creativity and maximize your multiple intelligences;

● understanding how the mind works and the implications of this;

● knowing how to seek out and use information, including through ICT;

● knowing how to communicate effectively in different ways.

This section outlines what the project has come to understand as learning style, how multiple intelligence approaches can contribute to creativity, and what the key operating principles of the mind are, along with some of the other approaches to learning that learners can acquire.

What do we mean by learning style?

I learn best when I'm allowed to talk to others and work within a group.

Pupils in 'Learning to learn' project school

The different approaches to completing the puzzle at the start of this chapter showed that we all have different ways of approaching our learning. Understanding these differences requires an understanding of learning styles. As you might expect, the teacher's awareness of different learning styles (including their own) has a critical impact on the pupil's learning.

It is sometimes unclear what we actually mean when we use the term 'learning style'. It can appear to be a synonym for different ability levels in traditional academic learning. For the purposes of the 'learning to learn' project, the Campaign has defined two key components to a person's learning style:

- how they prefer to take in information (visual, auditory or kinesthetic) and

- how they prefer to process that information and do their learning.

Taking in information

I learn best by doing something I enjoy so I remember, and I am better at doing something visual.

Pupil in 'learning to learn' project school

We take in information through our eyes, ears and bodies (by touching/doing things and by smelling and tasting things). Most of us do all these things, but equally most of us also have a preference for certain ways of taking in information as the following characters show.

Understanding these sensory preferences was one of the main areas of research conducted by the 'learning to learn' schools. The details of the findings are discussed in Chapter 5 and the project Research Report, and can be summarized as follows: pupils enjoy finding out about their sensory preferences and find it useful, with those that prefer taking in information kinesthetically benefiting in particular. Equally, pupils need to be aware of the chart on page 70, which shows that we take in and remember information best when we vary the sensory input. For teachers, perhaps the key point is that the best way of conveying information is to cover all the options.

Knowing about sensory preferences not only ensures that teachers get information across better, but also allows learners to adapt their learning strategies to how they prefer to take in that information. For example, a visual learner knows to use mind maps, and an auditory learner knows they might learn better while listening to music (or alternatively might learn worse, as it is more likely to distract their musical ear! See the Ogmore School case study on the effects of using music in the classroom on pages 102ff).

The skill of processing information

We are drowning in information but thirsting for knowledge.

Klas Mellander quoted in *From the ivory tower... to the street*,
Campaign for Learning conference report, 1996

The Klas Mellander quote above dates from 1996, but it is still very much true today. In our media-driven age we are bombarded with information. In workplaces we are expected to manage this overload increasingly quickly. Yet why should children have to remember the key dates of British history when they are available at the touch of a button? What we need today are the skills of information processing, synthesis, analysis and application in different contexts.

The questions that arise from this include: What knowledge and skills should be core in any school curriculum and which should be optional? How should pupils develop both depth and breadth in their learning? How might we future-proof the curriculum, preparing pupils for as yet unforeseen technological advances in the future? This is precisely where 'learning to learn' comes in, with learning to process information as a key component.

Working out your learning style

Having identified the way we prefer to take in information, we need to assess our preference for processing that information in order to work out our learning style. There are a number of approaches to assessing these preferences, although most of them are used more in workplaces than schools. One of the most popular was developed by psychologists Peter Honey and Alan Mumford and identifies people as:

- **activists**, who like to roll up their sleeves and get stuck in. They tend to act first and think later.
- **reflectors**, who like to absorb a range of data before coming to any decision.

- **theorists**, who like to think things through into a logical sequence and identify patterns, systems and rules.

- **pragmatists**, who like to experiment and test things out until they find the best way of doing things.

These categories do not necessarily correlate with specific ways of taking in information. For example you can be a theorist who prefers taking in information visually, or an auditory pragmatist. Based on this, in his book *Power up your Mind*, Bill Lucas gives the following simple equation for working out your learning style:

Understanding learning styles is critical for people in any walk of life. They allow people to learn better and handle information more effectively. Perhaps more importantly they allow people to communicate better with others because they recognize that different learning styles require different communication approaches. NLP (see box on page 62) offers many other techniques for communicating effectively with others.

Multiple intelligences and realizing your creative potential

The project was about learning differently and that's why it was good.

Year 9 pupil in 'learning to learn' project school

Ask most adults what 'intelligent' means to them and they will use words like 'brainy', 'good at school work' and 'clever'. For too long IQ, or Intellectual Quotient, has been the prevailing influence on theories of intelligence. It has made a single test which predominantly assesses our linguistic and mathematical abilities the defining factor in whether or not someone sees themselves as 'intelligent'. The effect of this has been to artificially inflate the importance of language and figures at the expense of other important forms of intelligence such as creativity, practical abilities, common sense or the ability to manage our emotions.

In reality we know that intelligence involves a combination of know-how as well as know-what across a multitude of contexts. Psychologist Professor Howard Gardner started a welcome revolution here when he first developed the idea of multiple intelligences. In the 1980s he started with seven, then introduced an eighth and is now toying with a ninth, existential intelligence. We think that there may be as many as ten: linguistic, mathematical, visual, physical, musical, environmental, emotional, social, practical and spiritual.

Emotional intelligence, which has been shown by the American author Daniel Goleman to be one of the most essential elements of success in the modern world, is included here for completeness but is a key element of Resilience, where it is essential for coping under stress.

case study

Prince William School

Northamptonshire, 13–18 Mixed Comprehensive Upper

Research area

Multiple intelligences

Hypothesis

Year 11 pupils who understand the concept of multiple intelligences will perform better in a block examination.

Research focus

Two matched Year 11 groups (target and comparison) studying RE

Methodology

A target group and a comparison group of Year 11 pupils, matched for ability and gender who were studying RE were selected for the project. The target group were specifically taught using the theory of multiple intelligences and it was incorporated and made explicit in the planning, teaching and assessment of the course. The comparison group were taught the usual course with the usual methods.

Success criteria

Better performance in an examination

Positive attitudes to learning and teaching

Key findings

The pupils in the target group reported a more positive approach to teaching and learning as well as more fun, enjoyment and opportunities to be creative.

The results for the mock examination were significantly higher in the target group. The average GCSE grade was 1.7 per cent higher than in the comparison group. The actual GCSE results showed a similar difference in performance.

A small number of traditionally academic pupils disliked the approach and thought that time was 'being wasted' when spent on ideas like multiple intelligences. One interpretation is that this group of pupils thought that the traditional advantages of being 'logic smart' or 'word smart' might be eroded.

Conclusions

The use of the theory of multiple intelligences with Year 11 pupils in RE allows pupils on the C/D border and below in particular to gain access to achievement. It enhances self-esteem and belief and motivates students by removing learning blocks set up by negative labelling or grouping policies.

Simply understanding the concept of multiple intelligences can be a liberating experience for many learners, helping to build their self-esteem and confidence when they realize that it is not a case of 'are you smart?' but of 'how are you smart?' However, identifying your intelligence strengths is only an important first step. It can sometimes appear that pupils are simply re-pigeon-holing themselves when they say 'I'm musical, linguistic' and then refuse to develop themselves in other areas. The real aim for a lifelong learner should be to develop yourself in as many areas as possible and so realize your full creative potential.

Of course there are many approaches to developing creativity, from learned techniques such as Edward de Bono's Six Thinking Hats to simply understanding that sometimes you need a break and a short walk to stimulate your ideas.

Different approaches to learning

The most important thing I learned this year is that there are lots of different ways of learning.

Pupil in 'learning to learn' project school

Resourcefulness also means having a toolkit of ideas and approaches for learning. These might be generic ways of learning, such as immersing yourself in an experience, learning in groups versus learning on your own, or trusting your intuition rather than always looking for logical, rational solutions. Equally, these may be more formal techniques, a few of which are listed below. The point is that effective lifelong learners think about which approaches to apply when and constantly seek to stretch their learning boundaries by searching out new approaches and experiences.

What is Neuro-Linguistic Programming (NLP)?

NLP is the study of the structure of subjective experience:

Neuro – the mind-body and how it works.

Linguistic – the language we use to describe and categorize our world and to make sense of experience.

Programming – sequences that repeat, patterns of thought and behaviour that help us or hinder us.

The approach has drawn on different strands of psychology and linguistics to build a simple set of practices that can assist learning and performance in all walks of life. Essentially NLP involves being clear about what you want and how you might best achieve your goal. NLP is particularly useful for helping learners to communicate effectively and is therefore useful for building Resourcefulness. It is widely used in the workplace, from coaching sports stars to helping advertising executives develop successful media campaigns.

Key text: *The Principles of NLP*, Joseph O'Connor and Ian McDermott, Thorsons, 1996

Creating a learning to learn school - *research and practice for raising standards, motivation and morale*

There are far too many learning techniques to be able to list them here, but many are included in the books in the Resources section at the back of this book. Well known examples include mind maps and brainstorming. NLP offers many other less well known but equally effective approaches, such as:

- feed-forward: a positive alternative to brainstorming. One individual states an issue or problem and members of the group suggest ideas for solving it beginning with 'You could...'. The individual thanks each contributor and when they have enough ideas they stop the session politely without indicating which ideas they will use.

- time-lines: using our past experiences to prepare for things in the future. Imagine time running through you and away into the distance. Think of something you are worried about having to do in the future, like taking an exam. Now think about what qualities or skills you will need to draw on to do well, for example, keeping calm, getting a sense of all the questions first, thinking logically, and so on. Now think of times in the past when you have demonstrated those qualities and step back along your time line to recapture how that felt, what you saw and what you heard. Go back to other times when you have demonstrated the other qualities you will need. When you have gathered all these experiences together, step forward to the time you will need to use them and let yourself feel, see and hear how easy it will be now that you have all the skills and qualities you need!

Resourcefulness is also about seeing how to make the most of the endless external resources available for learning in the world around us. Perhaps more than any other resource, ICT offers exciting tools and techniques for enhancing learning, from the internet as a source of information, to dialogue tools such as chatboards and discussion groups, to whole online 'learning to learn' courses such as CHAMPS at www.learntolearn.org.

Understanding how the mind works

Teachers commonly state that not enough time is spent during teacher training on understanding the key operating principles of the mind, yet there is growing evidence from cognitive neuroscience indicating that the brain's innumerable functions can all impact how we learn.

When teachers understand how the brain works and some of its critical functions, they are more able to capitalize on the brain's natural functions and processes in their approaches to teaching and therefore to improve learning effectiveness.

Five of the key operating principles of the mind that we described in *Teaching pupils how to learn* as concepts which teachers should try to address in their teaching are summarized below. These are explored in more detail in *Power up your mind* by Bill Lucas.

1. Exploration: the mind's capacity to continually explore and seek to make sense of experience. This explains why the best learning activities are those which children can start easily, but which are so deep no one can finish.

2. Connection: the mind's disposition for making creative connections between things. This is the source of many of history's greatest inventions.

3. Pattern making: the mind's disposition for looking for and creating patterns. This is developed in classrooms by many of the Thinking Skills programmes, see box on pages 74 and 75.

4. Imitation: our mind's love to model what we see. This explains why apprenticeship is perhaps the oldest and still one of the most effective ways of learning.

5. Balancing stress and challenge. This is based on our primordial fight or flight response to danger. The mind needs low stress and high challenge to maximize its learning and performance.

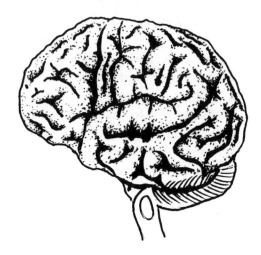

3. Resilience

I can always ask questions if I'm stuck and am not afraid to take part and say what I think.

Pupil in 'learning to learn' project school

Resilience is about keeping going with learning, having a go, knowing what to do when you are stuck and the other qualities and skills that can be seen in successful lifelong learners. The key areas can be summarized as:

- knowing how to apply learned optimism and self-efficacy approaches;

- understanding empathy and EQ approaches;

- knowing what to do when stuck; and

- knowing how to ask (critical) questions.

Perhaps more than any of the other 5 Rs of lifelong learning, Resilience is a deep-set attitude or disposition developed through early childhood experiences and over which schools can have limited influence. But it is possible to encourage it, both through the culture of the school and through practical approaches and techniques such as mentoring, Assessment for Learning and learned optimism. This section focuses on some of the approaches taken by the project schools to develop Resilience in pupils.

In *Wise up: the challenge of lifelong learning*, Professor Guy Claxton states the following:

Comprehension is not a process of adding little pieces of information one-by-one to an expanding structure of knowledge, or assembling "mastery" out of a regime of carefully defined and practised component skills. Much learning involves exhilarating spurts, frustrating plateaus and upsetting regressions. That's why Resilience is so important.

At the launch conference for the 'learning to learn' project's Phase 1 findings in May 2002, Claxton spoke about the effect that our modern world is having on children.

Open any serious Sunday broadsheet and you will be assailed by stories that reflect the fact that many teenagers today have lost their sense of belonging and purpose in the world: pregnancies, drugs, drink, truanting, violence. These and other manifestations necessitate all the more strongly the need to develop resilience.

Developing Resilience: practical approaches

If Readiness involves motivating yourself and having valued learning goals at the start of a learning experience, Resilience is about maintaining that motivation in the face of set-backs. Not surprisingly, many of the approaches for teachers outlined in the Readiness section hold true for developing Resilience. For example Assessment for Learning/Formative Assessment (see below) can break down what might otherwise appear as learning 'failure' into constructive feedback and indications of which approach to try next. Although broader than just Resilience, the *Myself as a Learner Scale* developed by Professor Bob Burden and published by nfer Nelson is a useful diagnostic tool for teachers wanting to assess how their pupils are feeling about their academic learning abilities, with useful pointers for how these can be developed.

What is Assessment for Learning/Formative Assessment?

The research indicates that improving learning through assessment depends on five deceptively simple key factors:

- the provision of effective feedback to pupils;
- the active involvement of pupils in their own learning;
- adjusting teaching to take account of the results of assessment;
- a recognition of the profound influence assessment has on the motivation and self-esteem of pupils, both of which are crucial influences on learning; and
- the need for pupils to be able to assess themselves and understand how to improve.

Assessment that promotes learning:
- is embedded in a view of teaching and learning of which it is an essential part;
- involves sharing learning goals with pupils;

- aims to help pupils to know and to recognize the standards they are aiming for;
- involves pupils in self-assessment;
- provides feedback which leads to pupils recognizing their next steps and how to take them;
- is underpinned by confidence that every student can improve; and
- involves both teacher and pupils reviewing and reflecting on assessment data.

The KMOFAP project, run by researchers at King's College London with teachers in schools in Medway and Oxfordshire, applied these principles to develop practical strategies for Formative Assessment. These include four distinct approaches:

- questioning: for example by using open questions and waiting longer for pupils to think before answering;
- feedback through marking: for example by not using grades, by only writing comments which identify what has been done well and what needs more work, and by setting out what pupils must do to follow up on and improve work;
- peer-assessment and self-assessment: for example by making the evaluation criteria transparent and asking pupils to assess and discuss one another's work in the light of these;
- the formative use of summative tests: for example by asking pupils to set their own questions and mark responses so that they can understand the assessment process and requirements.

Key texts: *Inside the black box, raising standards through classroom assessment*, Paul Black and Dylan William, Kings College London, 1998; *Assessment for Learning: beyond the black box*, Assessment Reform Group, 1999; *Working inside the black box: assessment for learning in the classroom*, Paul Black et al, 2002

In terms of the culture of the school, the way that success and failure are defined or perceived is critical. If exam results are clearly the one and only measure then, inevitably, some pupils will be losers and may choose instead to be 'good' at failing, by truanting or simply refusing to strive for success they do not believe is within their grasp.

But Resilience is not just for those on the academic borderline. Studies by Carol Dweck in America have shown that high-flying girls are perhaps most in need of it. When exam papers were altered to include impossible questions in the middle, it was the 'bright' girls who were most likely to fall apart faced by something at which they could not succeed, while other students moved on and completed the questions they could do. The other students were also more likely to have creative attempts at answering the impossible questions, suggesting that they would grow up to be far more effective problem solvers in our complex real world.

Resilient learners overcome the vicissitudes of learning with a range of strategies that range from sheer gritted teeth to learned optimism and self-belief and from asking other people for help to taking a break until they are ready to return to their learning. The 'learning to learn' schools and those involved in the ELLI project (see box on pages 82 and 83) have developed a number of approaches to developing pupils' resilience, such as the 'Top tips for what to do when you get stuck'.

Returning to the importance of the culture of the school, Resilience can be fostered in many more subtle ways. These include:

- involving parents in supporting learning through parent evenings, 'learning to learn' sessions and courses (see case study on Malet Lambert School in Hull on pages 108ff);

- introducing mentoring, including peer mentoring (see case study on Camborne School on pages 87ff); and

- actively developing peer group dynamics and commitment to real world learning within classes. Ellowes Hall School in Dudley allocated £150 to each class to spend on a learning activity of their choice, so long as it was developed collectively and democratically. *Citizenship schools: a practical guide to education for citizenship and personal development*, written by Titus Alexander and published by the Campaign includes many ideas for how citizenship can be experienced as well as taught in this way.

Resilience also involves the ability to ask critical questions, although this is strongly linked to effective Reflection when we look back on a learning experience and work out what we really feel and think, rather than what we were told to feel and think. Critical questioning is essential in the modern world, where information is universal but not always authentic. That said, it is one of the most challenging issues for teachers in developing 'learning to learn', since it involves them shifting from the role of 'sage on the stage' (who knows all the answers) to become co-learners seeking and evaluating possible answers with their pupils. Many Thinking Skills and Critical Skills courses exist which give practical tools for teachers to develop these and related skills.

Of course, great sensitivity is needed in questioning others and their sources of information. Despite the rhetoric of flat structures and learning organizations, workplaces (and society more generally) require a sophisticated awareness of when and how to question authority. This is why empathy and Emotional Intelligence (EQ) are included within Resilience. These skills are particularly needed when we are most challenged and under stress ourselves. Quality Circle Time is a widespread approach to developing these qualities, while Antidote (the organization that campaigns for Emotional Literacy) is developing a project looking at other EQ approaches.

What is Quality Circle Time ?

The Quality Circle Time Model has been developed by writer and thinker Jenny Mosley. It provides the means to establish an inclusive and ongoing process of school development through which a positive ethos is put in place for all members of the school community. Regular circle meetings, and the negotiation of clear ground rules for all adults and pupils ensure that specific relationship skills are taught and maintained; interpersonal issues are addressed and the celebration of success is built into the daily routines of every area of school life. The guiding principle is that people learn from each other. Teachers learn from pupils and pupils learn from each other and so on. The circle symbolizes the quality of opportunity for all people to create the right learning ethos in their team.

The following are the key elements in the Quality Circle Time model:

Weekly Circle Times incorporate games and exercises designed to foster a sense of 'team', enhance social and emotional skills, encourage the development of self-discipline and allow the class to act as responsible and caring citizens.

Bubble Time or Talk Time is a one-to-one listening systems available to all pupils.

Think Books are a daily non-verbal system for pupils who need to communicate in other ways such as drawing or writing.

Golden Rules are the means by which the values of Circle Time are extended into every area of school life. They enable children to become more aware of their rights to speak and their responsibility to listen.

Incentives is a system of rewards structured to reinforce the Golden Rules. The whole school community, including the children themselves, celebrate any social and emotional improvement by giving specific rewards and praise.

Privilege Time is a system of rewards for keeping the Golden Rules with a weekly privilege of enjoyable community play. This also acts as a motivational based system of sanctions as the privileges can be withdrawn.

Lunchtime Policy teaches children playground games and selects them to act as 'Playground Friends', to work with the teachers and midday supervisors to set up creative, safe playgrounds.

Children Beyond shows teacher how to initiate 'guaranteed success' programmes for children who are 'beyond' the usual motivational procedures. Circles of Support are set up as a therapeutic strategy for children needing intensive social skills or self-esteem building.

Circle Time Meetings are used to deliver all the above to policies by providing a group listening system for 'planning-doing and -reviewing'. They give all individuals a practical opportunity to discuss concerns, consider moral values, practise positive behaviours, and offer solutions to each other in a planned and sequential manner.

4. Remembering

(Mind maps) help us plan and remember things, (they) help me remember and it's easier to do than just writing things in lists.

Pupil in 'learning to learn' project school

The key elements of Remembering outlined in this section are:

- understanding different memory approaches
- understanding how to make connections
- understanding how to apply learning, including in different contexts.

Is learning simply memories that stick? If that is the case, why is it that we often seem to remember bizarrely inconsequential episodes from our past and yet forget what happened yesterday? Like many of the workings of the brain, memory is still only partly understood, but maximizing our control over it is essential for effective lifelong learning.

Every experience that we have leaves a trace of electrochemical connections between our synapses. But, of course, if we remembered every single experience we had we would rapidly reach sensory overload. So what is it that means some things stick and others do not? Two factors seem to influence whether a memory will stick in our mind or not:

- if it has meaning for us, for example it relates to something we are already interested in or is something we are very keen to remember (like a PIN or telephone number).
- if it fires our emotions in some way, explaining why we remember things like our first kiss (although overstressing our emotions produces chemicals which reduce our learning effectiveness).

The key principles of memory

From this and other research a number of key memory principles have been identified by thinkers such as Tony Buzan. Each of them has practical implications for both teachers and learners:

- We tend to remember the first and last items in a sequence, which is why Accelerated Learning lessons are chunked into short sections with brief review sessions at the end of each one.
- Finding the patterns and connections between things helps you to remember them, partly because your brain is stimulated in the process and also because we are 'hard wired' for stories which can be told and retold.
- We tend to remember things that stick out in our minds because they are surprising or odd.
- We remember things better when we review them periodically after we have learned them.

Mind maps draw on these and other memory principles. Drawing a mind map forces you to find patterns and hierarchies, while its visual impact and use of colour and pictures helps make the learning stick.

Other memory techniques include using mnemonics, for example by thinking of memorable acronyms to remember a series of words. An example of this is learning expert Colin Rose's MASTER learning cycle, which stands for:

Mind relaxed

Acquire the facts

Search out the meaning

Trigger the memory

Exhibit what you know

Reflect on the process

Perhaps the most important factor of all for effective memory storage is the need to reinforce learning by accessing it through all our senses. This doubly reinforces the point made in the Learning Styles section above that a good teacher will present information in a range of different ways. After all:

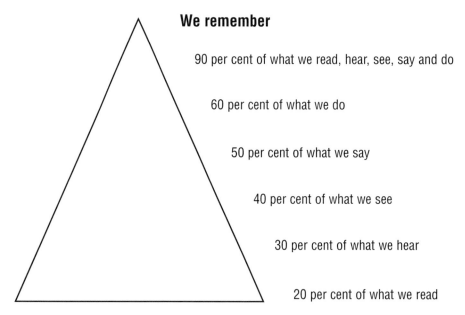

We remember

90 per cent of what we read, hear, see, say and do

60 per cent of what we do

50 per cent of what we say

40 per cent of what we see

30 per cent of what we hear

20 per cent of what we read

As Alistair Smith has noted, this is why pupils in 'learning to learn' schools will look up during tests at the spot on the walls where their revision posters had been pinned. Others might be seen retracing the path of the atom they had taken during a kinesthetic science lesson!

Finally of course, it is often said that the best way to internalize and remember something is to teach it to someone else. Applying learning is a key skill for Remembering, not only because it makes it real and practical, but also because it helps us to remember. Many of the 'learning to learn' schools used peer teaching to enhance understanding and memory for exactly this reason.

Applying what you have learned

A more difficult, but equally essential skill, is knowing how to apply learning in different contexts. This is often known as transfer, although this may be an unhelpful term since it is rare that we can directly transfer something learned in one sphere directly to another. It might be true of using fractions in both science and maths, but when it comes to lifelong learning techniques we will more often need to adapt and effectively relearn things in different contexts, even if we are drawing on skills and techniques learned elsewhere. This issue raises the difficult question of whether 'learning to learn' approaches are best taught as a separate subject or embedded within the mainstream curriculum. It is returned to in Chapter 6, but it is worth stating here 'learning to learn' approaches certainly need to be reinforced and modelled in a range of contexts and curriculum areas to truly make them effective.

Reflectiveness

'Learning to learn' has helped the pupils at our school to reflect on how they learn and to begin to understand themselves as learners.

Teacher in 'learning to learn' project school

The final R is perhaps the one that is least well catered for in many busy classrooms. Essentially Reflectiveness involves knowing how to:

- stop,
- reflect (e.g. ask questions, observe, see patterns),
- experiment and
- evaluate learning.

The Ready, Go, Steady model of learning outlined in the Readiness section deliberately highlights the fact that we often focus too little attention on the Steady stage, when we should reflect on what and how we have learned. Developing Reflectiveness is hugely important for the other four Rs. It is the point when learners look back at what and how they have learned, which helps imprint onto our long-term memory and builds critical thinking for the future. It is also important itself: simply taking time to sit back and clear our conscious minds so that our thoughts can crystallize is hugely valuable and often leads to our most creative new ideas. As with all other areas of 'learning to learn', teachers need to model Reflectiveness and create time, opportunities and a language for doing it.

case study

Cornwallis School

Kent, 11–18 Mixed Comprehensive

Research area

'Learning to learn' strategies in science in Year 9

Hypothesis

Learning strategies have an impact on student motivation and attainment in science in Year 9 at Cornwallis School.

Research focus

A group of 25 Year 9 pupils with higher ability in science who were compared with a comparison group of the same size and ability

Methodology

Pupils in the target group were introduced to 'learning to learn' strategies that included Brain Gym®, ICT (e.g. digital video authoring), the use of music, learning styles, thinking skills, multiple intelligences and EQ (emotional intelligence).

Both groups were monitored throughout the year using:

- pre- and post-tests to check for improvement
- performance monitoring in examinations e.g. mock assessment tests
- baseline data including CAT scores to check value added performance during the year, key stage and differences between the groups.

Questionnaires and interviews were used to monitor motivation.

The project ended before assessment tests. Quantitative and qualitative data were collected.

Success criteria

Higher attainment levels

Increased motivation

Key findings

Although pupils in the comparison group achieved as well as or better than the target group in some of the measures (e.g. average KS2 level, per cent of level 5 at KS2), those in the target group displayed significant improvements between pre- and post-tests (18 per cent vs 1.6 per cent). The average level of improvement during Year 9 was assessed as 1.0 for the target group vs 0.4 for the comparison group.

In relation to levels of motivation:

- 65 per cent of the target group reported that they enjoyed science (vs 0 per cent of the comparison group);

- 85 per cent of the target group reported that they learned a lot in science lessons (vs 52.3 per cent for the comparison group); and

- 55 per cent of the target group reported that they learned a lot in school lessons (vs 36.4 per cent of the comparison group).

Conclusions

Pupils in the target group made greater progress during the year relative to other pupils. Specifically, they improved the most from pre-test to post-test and their final improvement was several percentages higher than the comparison group. Greater improvement in this group suggests that the learning strategies employed by the pupils had an impact on their attainment.

Pupils also indicated that they learned best when they enjoyed themselves or had fun, indicating that their emotional state is fundamental to learning. The use of learning strategies helped increase enjoyment and consequently the motivation of pupils in the target group.

Qualitative data suggested that the ethos underpinning the 'learning to learn' approach permeated all lessons, including those using new technologies. ICT strategies can not only enhance the learning experience but can also develop Innovation, Creativity and Thinking (cf ICT) often found to be missing in science as well as other subjects.

Managing reflection in class

One of the key opportunities for this is the plenary session, at the end of a learning section or lesson. These sessions serve many purposes: from creating a sense of achievement by taking stock and reiterating what has been learned; to helping pupils draw out the applications of the learning and think through how they could communicate it to someone else; to giving the teacher feedback on how far pupils have achieved the learning objectives so they can plan forward. Critically, they are also an opportunity to take the learning further and deeper and to prompt deep thinking by pupils about how they have learned, so instilling the habit of reflection and helping pupils develop a perception of themselves as learners. The Foundation Subjects materials developed for the Key Stage 3 Strategy contain many excellent examples and video clips of how teachers can manage effective plenaries (as well as many of the other 'learning to learn' approaches).

What are Thinking Skills?

A range of different Thinking Skills approaches have been developed and many of these are well known in schools. Some examples are:

- Feuerstein's Instrumental Enrichment
- Somerset Thinking Skills
- Philosophy for Children
- CASE (Cognitive Acceleration through Science Education), CAME (Cognitive Acceleration through Maths Education) and CATE (Cognitive Acceleration through Technology Education)
- Thinking through… Geography
- ACTS (Activating Children's Thinking Skills).

Many of the approaches have been evaluated and shown to have a significant impact on standards, for example CASE succeeded in raising pupil's grades in GCSEs (on average one grade) two to three years after the programme had been completed.

A review of Thinking Skills approaches by Carol McGuiness, of Queen's University, Belfast, for the DfES has identified a number of core concepts between the various approaches:

- Learning is about searching out meaning and imposing structure
- Focusing on thinking skills in the classroom is important because it equips pupils to go beyond the information given, to deal systematically yet flexibly with novel problems and situations, to adopt a critical attitude to information and argument as well as to communicate effectively.
- If students are to become better thinkers they need to be taught explicitly how to do it.

- Acquiring and using metacognitive skills has emerged as a powerful idea for promoting a thinking skills curriculum.
- Children bring their own conceptions (and misconceptions) into the classroom.
- Developing better thinking and reasoning skills may have as much to do with creating dispositions for good thinking as it has to do with acquiring specific skills and strategies.

Key text: From *Thinking skills to thinking classrooms*, Carol McGuinness, DfES

The Foundation Subjects materials also include more general approaches to developing Reflectiveness, many of them drawing on Thinking Skills approaches. The following dialogue is from a Year 8 geography class plenary session. The class had been studying a mystery (a Thinking Skills approach which involves posing pupils with one big open question and giving them a range of data on small slips of paper which they must use to answer the question) about tensions and problems in inner city areas. In the plenary they are asked to identify the assumptions they have made in deciding who smashed a car windscreen, on the basis of incomplete evidence.

T	What do you think you learned during that lesson?
MP1	We learned about assumptions, like you shouldn't just rush into deciding something without thinking carefully.
MP2	Yeah, you thought you were right and then you had to think about it and you weren't so sure, especially when you listened to other groups.
Int	How did the teacher help you?
FP1	The teacher kept saying, 'Do you really know that?' Is it a fact?' Usually we were wrong, well, sort of.
MP2	You had to have evidence to back it up, like in a court...a trial.
FP1	At the end you see how lots of fights start. People think they are right, but they don't think, not really. It was funny when the teacher talked about fights he used to have with his brother, just like me and my sister.

(T = teacher; MP = male pupil; FP = female pupil; Int = interviewer)

The dialogue illustrates perfectly how reflection helps crystallize thinking, but how its success depends on well constructed learning activities and teachers modelling learning and challenging pupils to justify their arguments and make their thinking transparent.

There are many other tools for building Reflectiveness that pupils can learn to use whether in or out of class. Keeping a learning diary, drawing mind maps at the end of a learning experience to capture your thoughts, telling your version of the story to someone else, talking about good and bad moments, being coached by a peer and writing a report are just some of these.

Developing the 5 Rs: a new role for teachers

The 5 Rs approach set out in this chapter has far-reaching implications for how teachers teach, from how they present information to how they use a learning model to structure learning, to how they plan lessons to develop the 5 Rs. This section sets out how teachers might view their role in developing the 5 Rs for lifelong learning. It describes Guy Claxton's model for the role of the teacher and highlights some of the difficulties teachers may encounter in adopting such a role, in particular in changing their perceptions of pupils' ability.

In *Building Learning Power*, Guy Claxton argues that teachers should always think simultaneously about how they will get a concept across and build Learning Power (see box on pages 82 and 83). Their role should be as a Team Coach, setting and holding a vision of what the learning is for, encouraging pupils to keep going, building a team atmosphere and communities of enquiry in the classroom, celebrating pupil achievements, and setting individual targets for improving performance.

Explaining	**Telling pupils directly and explicitly about learning power (or the 5 Rs)**
Informing	Making clear the overall purpose of the classroom
Reminding	Offering ongoing reminders and prompts about learning power (or the 5 Rs)
Discussing	Inviting pupils' own ideas and opinions about learning
Training	Giving direct information and practice in learning: tips and techniques
Commentating	**Conveying messages about learning power (or the 5 Rs) through informal talk and formal and informal evaluation**
Nudging	Drawing individual pupils' attention towards their own learning
Replying	Responding to pupils' comments and questions in ways that encourage 'learning to learn'
Evaluating	Commenting on difficulties and achievements in learning-positive ways
Tracking	Recording the development of pupils' learning power (or 5 Rs)
Orchestrating	**Selecting activities and arranging the environment**
Selecting	Choosing activities that develop the 4/5 Rs
Framing	Clarifying the learning intentions behind specific activities
Target setting	Helping students set and monitor their own learning power/5 Rs targets
Arranging	Making use of displays and physical arrangements to encourage independence

Modelling	Showing what it means to be an effective learner
Reacting	Responding to unforeseen events, questions etc. in ways that model good learning
Learning aloud	Externalizing the thinking, feeling and decision making of a learner in action
Demonstrating	Having learning projects that are visible in the classroom
Sharing	Talking about their own learning careers and histories

The challenge of changing practice

The difficulty of teachers genuinely transforming their practice in this way should not be underestimated. Many of the project schools stated that, initially at least, 'learning to learn' approaches can require more work, and almost all of them had difficulty in persuading some of their colleagues to adopt the approaches. This section highlights some of these difficulties and points to some of the deep-seated cultural assumptions that influence many teachers' professional activities and that may need to be challenged in developing school-wide 'learning to learn' approaches.

David Leat's experience of working with teachers introducing Thinking Skills approaches allows him to emphasize the difficulties they face:

Individual teachers face some difficult challenges in introducing Thinking Skills programmes. They require a conceptualization of teaching and their subject(s) that accommodates an emphasis on developing learning skills, reasoning patterns and transfer. They have to be determined enough to overcome any resistance from their pupils. They need to establish a classroom discourse which encourages pupils to initiate, speculate and accept that there is not one right answer. They need to maintain this style when there may be pressures to be more didactic and they need to be able to defend and justify their approach in the face of scepticism, indifference and ignorance.

Dr David Leat, *Rolling the stone uphill: teacher development and the implementation of Thinking Skills programmes*, **Oxford Review of Education, Vol 25, No 3, 1999**

Arguably, it was the over-hasty introduction in the 1960s of what came to be called progressive Plowdenite methods of child-centred learning without sufficient support for those teachers who most needed it that led to the widespread perception that the reforms themselves had failed and the subsequent backlash towards more didactic methods.

International research has highlighted some interesting differences in teaching and learning approaches in different cultures. While this may represent a challenge if we are to change the UK culture, it also provides some inspirational models as the highly respected American academic Harold Stevenson suggests:

I visited a class (in Japan) where they were learning about Iceland... the teacher wasn't standing up there telling them all the derivatives of the questions that might be raised about Iceland. But by the time they ended the lesson, which lasted three days, they had created the geography of Iceland, the products of Iceland and so on. The main thing I think... the goal is not to transmit information from this authority figure of the teacher to the child. The goal is to elicit reactions from the child, which the teacher can then integrate and it's a production. The successful lesson is not one that everybody has come up with the same predetermined correct answer, but one in which the children have really thought about Iceland and what it is to live there.

Dr Harold Stevenson, Transcript from *Lessons from the world:*
***Stigler and Stevenson on TIMSS and Instruction*, 1997**

'Learning to learn' approaches have far stronger theoretical and research bases than the earlier Plowden reforms. Nevertheless, the challenge of transforming teacher's practice should not be underestimated. It has been explored throughout Phase 1 and 2 of the project, with one of the key findings being that teachers in departments that are already performing less well are less likely to improve as fast through 'learning to learn' approaches as those that are already performing well. Exploring how this finding can be countered is one of the key reasons for developing Phase 3 of the 'learning to learn' project.

Conclusion

This section has outlined:

- the key elements of 'learning to learn' and the 5 Rs for lifelong learning;
- ways in which schools and teachers can develop these;
- some of the specific approaches already available that schools can draw on in developing 'learning to learn'.

We believe that the elements of 'learning to learn' outlined here lead to an inevitable conclusion about what is important in schools – a reversal of the curriculum priorities so that the development of positive lifelong learning attitudes/attributes becomes the primary goal of education.

In the last two decades of the twentieth century, following the introduction of the National Curriculum, success has increasingly been defined by subject Knowledge (measured through exam performance tables). Skills are seen as important and Attitudes to learning less so. This is the KSA world that dominates formal schooling.

If you believe in 'learning to learn' then you are likely to want to reverse these priorities. You will prefer an ASK approach, where attitudes – we might even say Attributes – are most important, then Skills and last of all Knowledge. This is why we have framed the new 5 Rs for lifelong learning in this way.

Knowledge is important. Indeed you cannot see complex patterns and inter-relationships between elements without it. Nor can you determine what is subtle and original if you have little knowledge. But if schools and teachers want to help pupils become effective lifelong learners, their focus should be on developing attitudes and attributes rather than acquiring knowledge. The advantage of this approach, as shown by the research findings in Chapter 5, is that it can also help raise standards.

What the results also indicate is that a 'learning to learn' approach can also help raise teacher motivation. Teaching becomes an empowering means of creating and supporting a learning culture in a school and much less a process of transmitting (centrally prescribed) information and skills. In the process, the learning baton is passed to the pupil to become an independent learner for life.

Finally, a point worth noting is how valuable the 'learning to learn' project schools have found actually conducting the research as a way of forcing them to think about and reflect on what and how they have learned. Equally, when interviewed for this book, many headteachers commented that they found the process helpful in thinking through what they had done and how. Developing a research ethos in schools is a useful way in itself of developing and modelling a 'learning to learn' approach.

Creating a learning to learn school - *research and practice for raising standards, motivation and morale*

About the 'learning to learn' research project

As a member of the project Advisory Board and mentor to one of the project schools I have seen that this project is not only well run, but that it is making a real impact in terms of teacher motivation and morale as well as effective pupil learning. I expect it to have a significant influence on wider policy in the years ahead.

Judy Sebba, Senior Educational Advisor for Research, Standards and Effectiveness Unit, Department for Education and Skills

The focus of the national project

This chapter describes the two-year 'learning to learn' research project co-ordinated by the Campaign for Learning. The research took place in 25 schools throughout England and Wales between September 2000 and July 2002 and involved teacher-led professional enquiry within an overarching research framework. The findings from the two years of research are summarized in Chapter 5 and are described in more detail in the Phase 1 (September 2000 – July 2001) and Phase 2 (September 2001 – July 2002) Research Reports by Dr Jill Rodd. The research reports also describe the project's research approach in more detail and are available on www.campaign-for-learning.org.uk.

The 'learning to learn' research was designed to explore whether, and if so how, different 'learning to learn' approaches can help raise standards and create confident and effective lifelong learners. Other areas of interest included the impact of 'learning to learn' approaches on:

- teacher effectiveness, professional development and motivation;
- the development of pupils as independent learners;
- the involvement of parents; and
- school culture.

The key research question underpinning the research was: How can we help pupils to learn most effectively and so give each one the best chance to achieve his or her full potential?

As outlined in Chapter 3, the hypothesis underlying the research was that learning is learnable and that, if done successfully, the process of learning has a measurable impact on standards and motivation to learn. It is worth repeating that the thinking on how best to do this evolved over the course of the project in the light of the schools' practice and reflection. This evolution is seen as part and parcel of school-based professional enquiry and is one of the advantages of this research approach. The evolution can be seen visually in the differences between the two mind maps developed at the start of Phase 1 and Phase 2.

Inevitably, it was recognized that, without a longitudinal study, it was not possible to draw any conclusive evidence for the effects of 'learning to learn' on the development of lifelong learners, although indicative factors such as pupil motivation and transfer were assessed. Phase 3 of the project, which will involve working with a larger number of schools over three years and which is outlined in more detail in the box on page 96, will explore these issues in more depth.

About the project schools

The schools involved in the project were selected on the basis of research proposals designed and submitted by them. Over 200 applications were received by the Campaign from interested schools, from which 24 were selected to participate in the first year (Phase 1) of the research. 22 of these schools submitted research reports at the end of Phase 1, and 17 went on to participate in the second year of the research (Phase 2). One additional school was invited to join the project in the second year as it was already conducting complementary research as part of the ELLI project (see box below for details) and thus provided a structural link between these complementary initiatives.

The schools were deliberately selected as representative of the wider schools population. For example, they included schools:

- in the bottom five per cent for Key Stage 1 results,

- where approximately one-third of pupils are on the Special Needs Register,

- where one-third of pupils have an ethnic minority background, and

- where significant numbers of pupils entered the school with a reading age below their chronological age.

Equally, as the list of awards and achievements by some of the schools in Chapter 1 shows, many have achieved a huge amount over the course of the project.

What is the ELLI (The Effective Learning Power Profile) project?

The ELLI project has been co-ordinated by Professor Patricia Broadfoot, Professor Guy Claxton and Dr Ruth Deakin Crick at Bristol University's Graduate School of Education. The project identified seven underlying dimensions to Learning Power from a study that included over 1,600 learners from the age of seven to 25. These dimensions represent the ways in which learners are energized to think, feel and behave in learning situations:

- Growth orientation: a commitment to growth and change over time
- Meaning making: the capacity to make personally meaningful connections
- Critical curiosity: the tendency to want to get below the surface and find things out

- Creativity: the capacity to use imagination, playfulness and intuition
- Learning relationships: being able to learn with and from other people
- Strategic awareness: the capacity to be aware of how learning is happening
- Dependence and fragility: the contrast to all the positive dimensions.

The Effective Learning Power Profile includes a range of assessment tools that can be used to track and develop these aspects of Learning Power. The ELLI project has involved working with a group of schools (including one of the 'learning to learn' project schools) to explore how the Learning Power dimensions could be developed within the classroom.

Sixteen teachers used the Effective Learning Power Profiles with their classes to identify which aspects of Learning Power they would focus on developing. They then integrated the chosen Learning Power Dimensions into their learning objectives and after two terms, the children were assessed again to see if their Learning Power Profile had changed. The classes showed significant increases on the positive Learning Power Dimensions and had also reduced their profiles on fragility and dependence. However, in control classes matched to the experimental group where there were no Learning Power interventions, the Learning Power Profile actually decreased over the course of the year.

Key text: Guy Claxton, *Building Learning Power*, 2002

Overall the 25 schools involved included 16 secondary schools and nine primary schools, four of which focused on Nursery and Reception pupils. Two schools were in Wales and the remainder were spread throughout England. The schools were:

Ashgate Nursery School, Derby, Derbyshire*

Camborne School and Community College, Cornwall*

Campion School, Northamptonshire*

Cornwallis School, Maidstone, Kent*

Christ Church Primary School, Wiltshire**

Cramlington Community High School, Northumberland*

Ellowes Hall School, Dudley, West Midlands*

George Spencer School, Stapleford, Nottinghamshire+

Henry Beaufort School, Winchester, Hampshire+

Hipsburn County First School, Lesbury, Northumberland*

Kingdown School, Warminster, Wiltshire*

King James School, Knaresborough, North Yorkshire+

Ladysmith First School, Exeter, Devon*

Lytham St Anne's High Technology College, Lancashire+

Key:
+ = schools that participated in Phase 1 only; * = schools that participated in Phases 1 and 2; ** = school that participated in Phase 2 only.

Malet Lambert School, Hull*

Mortimer Comprehensive, Tyne and Wear+

Ogmore School, Bridgend, South Wales*

Prince William School, Peterborough*

Sandwich Technology School, Sandwich, Kent*

St. John's CE Primary, Salford, Greater Manchester+

Summerhill School, Kingswinford, West Midlands*

Tapton School, Sheffield+

Tasker Milward School, Haverfordwest, Pembrokeshire, Wales+

West Grove Primary School, Southgate, London*

Westwood Park Primary School, Salford, Greater Manchester +

Key:
+ = schools that participated in Phase 1 only; * = schools that participated in Phases 1 and 2; ** = school that participated in Phase 2 only.

Why did some schools drop out?

The factors that prevented seven of the original schools from continuing or reporting on their involvement with the project in the second year indicate the very real pressures on schools which can prevent them from developing. The reasons given included:

- changes in staffing,
- lack of funds to attend professional development events and provide cover for research staff to carry out research,
- changes in school agendas and directions,
- opportunities to join local research groups and networks,
- inability to implement research plans and methodologies,
- insufficient progress with their research, and
- lack of commitment by Senior Management Teams to the project.

Some of the staff in these schools continued to pursue research into 'learning to learn' independently but their findings are not included here. Another two of the original schools conducted research related to the project during 2001–2002, but the teachers involved were not able to submit reports due to pressures of work. Consequently, these schools have not been identified as 'learning to learn' schools for Phase 2 and their research has not been included in this report.

Who did what? How the project worked

The Campaign for Learning established and co-ordinated the project. This included raising funds; appointing a Research Leader (Jill Rodd), a Project Manager (Toby Greany), part-time Project Co-ordinator (Andrew Quinlan) and part-time seconded Schools Liaison Officer (Ray Wicks); selecting the schools; servicing the Advisory Board; running the Professional Development events for schools; disseminating the findings; taking forward the recommendations and proposals that emerged.

Advisory Board: A high-level Advisory Board made up of academics, leading thinkers, practitioners, civil servants and partner bodies oversaw the design, implementation and evaluation of the project. The research process itself was managed and evaluated by Dr Jill Rodd, an independent academic and educational consultant.

Research Leader: Dr Rodd worked with the Advisory Board and Campaign team to develop the research framework and support the project schools to carry out their research, through training, school visits and telephone/email support. She synthesized the findings and produced the research reports at the end of each phase.

Campaign for Learning

Schools: Each project school appointed a lead research manager who co-ordinated their project internally and was responsible for drawing together the findings. All schools involved teams of teachers in implementing the research, although the size of these varied from single departments to all staff. The staff involved attended professional development events run by the Campaign, developed research hypotheses and evaluation approaches in consultation with Jill Rodd, implemented the 'learning to learn' initiatives and collected data on impact. Each school was required to produce a short report outlining their findings at the end of each phase.

The research approach

The research involved school-based professional enquiry, often known as action research. The key roles of each of the project participants is set out in the diagram above. The case studies of the specific research approach and findings from individual schools given throughout this book illustrate the approach.

Each school designed its own research project within an overarching framework developed by the Campaign. In Phase 1 the schools were given the mind map on page 44 and asked to select specific areas for research within this that they would like to explore and which might cast light on the ways pupils learn. Before the start of Phase 2 the schools reviewed the content of the original mind map and developed the mind map on page 45 as the overall framework for this phase. They were then asked to:

1. Define their research hypothesis. For example, 'Do young children display more positive attitudes to learning and improved performance if their learning styles are taken into consideration by teachers?'

2. Develop an approach for how teachers would implement the research. For example, 'In which lessons? What development will teachers need? etc.'

3. Define indicators of success for measuring whether the hypothesis has been met (a template was developed with the schools to assist in this). For example, 'What do we mean by 'positive attitudes to learning' and to what extent should they change? Do we need target and control groups to evaluate the difference that the 'learning to learn' interventions make?'

4. Agree the data needed to measure the indicators of success. For example, pre/post questionnaires for pupils, national tests scores, GCSE results, Ofsted reports, etc.

5. Implement their approach.

6. Gather the data and report on the project according to a standard format.

There are many advantages to using this professional enquiry approach for the project, as it serves to pull out findings based in real-life school contexts. In the process it is highly developmental for the teachers involved because it:

- leads to cycles of questioning, answer seeking and reflection;

- encourages open-mindedness and a willingness to seek out and take account of various views;

- encourages commitment to and the valuing of work in schools and its improvement; and

- encourages responsibility for professional development in the short- and long-term.

Creating a learning to learn school - research and practice for raising standards, motivation and morale

Camborne School and Community College

Cornwall, 11–18 Mixed Comprehensive

Research area

1:1 Mentoring Programme for underachieving pupils in Years 10 and 11 that builds on the 'learning to learn' work from Phase 1

Hypotheses

Working with a mentor trained in 'learning to learn' approaches will benefit the learning of the current cohort of Year 10–11 pupils.

Gender biases in the appropriateness of methods used in the mentoring programme produce different responsiveness in girls compared to boys.

The attitudes of subject teachers can help or hinder the success of the mentoring programme.

The work of the appointed Learning Co-ordinator will result in improved attitudes, practice and attainment in pupils and be beneficial for parents and teachers.

Research focus

25 Year 10–11 pupils (12 boys and 13 girls) who were identified by teachers as significantly underachieving were selected to take part in the 1:1 Mentoring Programme

Methodology

A group of teachers were trained in Neuro-Linguistic Programming (see box on page 62) in order to improve skill and confidence to act as mentors for pupils. Specifically, the mentors addressed pupil underachievement that resulted from a negative self-image by examining internal and external barriers to learning and finding ways of overcoming them as well as working with pupils who had crises of confidence and self-belief at critical moments by developing positive anchors to help them take the next step. Pupil performance at GCSE was analysed in relation to the mentoring programme.

Year 11 pupils completed a questionnaire about the 'learning to learn' programme at two points in the year.

Teaching staff were surveyed about the value and impact of the Learning Co-ordinator role.

Success criteria

- Improvements in predicted GCSE results based on KS3 assessment tests scores.
- Percentage of the cohort who achieved or exceeded their predicted grades.
- Positive outcomes on attitudes and practices of teachers and parents.

Key findings

■ Of the 243 subject entries, pupils hit their target grades 85 times and exceeded them 61 times.

■ In 60 per cent of the exams taken by this cohort of students, the pupils hit or exceeded their target grade (compared to the 50 per cent of the average school population expected to hit or exceed predicted grades).

Case study analyses of two individual pupils illustrate the qualitative effects of the mentoring programme.

Boy A was recommended by nine of his teachers including the Year Head and his Form Tutor. He had been a constant concern throughout Years 9 and 10 and his parents were very worried about him, his attitude to school and his likely underachievement at GCSE. The mentoring programme addressed his feelings of being undervalued and of school experiences being irrelevant to him by focusing on moments in his school life where he received acclaim. These became his positive anchors. He was taught how to recall the positive feelings he had about himself through simple physical triggers. His self-belief began to reappear; subtle signals such as eye contact, concern for his appearance and attendance began to improve. At GCSE, he scored 9 A*-C grades, including 1A*, 3As and 4Bs. He has started AS courses at the school.

Girl B was referred to the programme because colleagues thought that her chronic shyness was significantly hampering her performance in school. She avoided contact with teachers, could not seek help and was a source of great concern to her friends and teachers. After a number of sessions that looked at her dreams for the future, her personal organization and stresses in her life, she asked for help in overcoming shyness which she acknowledged was a significant barrier to her success in and out of school. A range of approaches was tried, including rational analysis of her fears and addressing negative memories that she was bringing to any school situations; however, it was focusing on one major area of success in her life outside school that unlocked her potential. Ultimately, she hit or exceeded her targets in 70 per cent of her exams. Moreover, the last four months of school were joyful for her as she was able to take part in school life, establish some powerful friendships, discover the ability to talk to her father and manage to apply for and hold down a weekend job, in which she gained promotion during the summer. She thinks that the work done on the mentoring programme had a great deal to do with her success.

Gauging the impact of other factors on performance

This cohort of pupils had experienced the 'learning to learn' programme since Year 8. This included:

■ Super Learning Days for the whole year group

■ tutorial sessions on learning techniques

■ revision workshops, support with planning revised timetables

■ out of hours revision sessions and support from Form Tutors as mentors and

■ parents sessions in Years 9, 10, 11 on 'learning to learn' encouraging them to become involved in and supporting the learning process at home.

Analyses indicate that departments which take and seriously apply the 'learning to learn' agenda and principles are those in which student performance is higher than school average (for example, English 50.5 per cent A*-C, history 44 per cent A*-C). Those departments in which there has been active resistance to 'learning to learn' are those in which performance remains significantly below average (for example, design technology 18 per cent A*-C; PE GCSE 17 per cent A*-C). This data indicate that results are better in areas of the school where teachers actively think about pedagogy.

The 'learning to learn' programme was independently assessed by a group of Sixth Form pupils as part of a General Studies coursework assignment. Thirty Year 11 pupils were randomly selected and invited to complete a questionnaire at two points in the year. The results from this small sample indicated that:

■ 67 per cent of the pupils thought it was very important to take part in 'learning to learn' sessions

■ 70 per cent of the pupils thought that 'learning to learn' affected the way that they worked at home and at school and they used the ideas from sessions most of the time

■ 71 per cent thought that 'learning to learn' should be part of the regular school timetable

■ The techniques used most were:

    making posters and diagrams (62 per cent)

    using music to help concentration (62 per cent)

    relaxation (56 per cent)

    mind mapping (44 per cent)

    putting up posters around the room (43 per cent)

    working with a friend (35 per cent)

    testing myself (28 per cent)

    using memory tricks e.g. mnemonics (20 per cent)

How could the mentoring programme be restructured to meet the needs of those students who did not respond to it?

The mentoring programme dealt well with students who:

■ had never before articulated their ambitions;

■ had low self-esteem;

■ had parents who are pushy and nagging;

■ just needed organizing; and

■ simply needed someone on whom to offload their confused feelings.

The mentoring programme dealt less effectively with students who:

■ had already firmly adopted life styles and values (for example, regular soft drug use with parental consent/regular non-attendance with parental support);

- received minimal support from home; and

- had teachers who are less positive about 'learning to learn'.

Plans to deal more effectively with such students in the future include:

- appointing an Advanced Skills Teacher (AST) whose responsibilities will include involving parents to a greater extent in the education of their children, stimulating ambition and aspiration within the community and bridging the gulf between home and school;

- further staff training in Neuro-Linguistic Programming;

- the appointment of Year Achievement Co-ordinators to take the mentoring programme into each year from 7 to 13.

Is there a gender bias in the appropriateness of methods used in the mentoring programme?

The data suggested that methods used in mentoring are appropriate to both boys and girls. Boys hit or exceeded their targets in 61 per cent of the exams while girls hit or exceeded their targets in 59 per cent. However, the content of the mentoring sessions was slightly differentiated to take account of gender differences, with the mentoring of boys placing a greater emphasis on:

- intervention with individual staff to create more flexible deadlines and to break large tasks into smaller, more manageable pieces;

- greater encouragement of boys to use ICT to help them learn (for example, boys used Mind Manager Mind Mapping software more than girls);

- material changes in sessions dealing with motivation (visualization of the future) (for example, 'What sort of car do you have at the age of 25?');

- reminding boys about sessions;

- contact with parents of boys (on average two letters and two phone calls to boys' parents compared to an average of one of each for girls' parents);

- practical support (for example, 'Let's go out and buy that book right now'; 'Let's get back to Mum's place and sort the computer out now').

Did the attitudes of some subject teachers help or hinder the success of the mentoring programme?

It was very clear that the combination of teachers was a key factor in determining student attitude to subjects, schoolwork and education in general. It became obvious that there were A and B teams in certain subjects and it was possible to predict with some accuracy those areas in which pupils were likely to be performing and those in which there would be difficulties. Informal conversations and interviews with pupils revealed that those who had a combination of teachers who were flexible, open minded, willing to experiment and embrace change were happier and performed better. Where teacher characteristics included rigidity, 'doing it this way because this is how it always has been done', pupils expressed less contentment and on balance found the subjects more difficult to master.

Creating a learning to learn school - *research and practice for raising standards, motivation and morale*

Did the intervention of a dedicated school-based Learning Co-ordinator benefit attitudes, practice and attainment for pupils, parents and teachers?

The Learning Co-ordinator role has been in place for two years. In that time the following initiatives have been put in place:

- 1:1 Mentoring Programme with Year 11 GCSE pupils;
- 'learning to learn' programmes for all pupils in Years 7 through to 13;
- 'learning to learn' programmes for all parents in those year groups;
- regular learning matters newsletter to all staff;
- in-service training in 'learning to learn' in school for NQTs and ITT students;
- establishment of an in-school Learning Forum, with regular termly meetings to discuss and share good practice;
- the establishment of good links with the University of the First Age (UFA);
- UFA summer schools in 2001 and 2002;
- brainwave 2002, experimenting with what a school of the future might look like;
- out-of-hours learning initiatives based on a Learnacy agenda funded by the UFA;
- the Learning Co-ordinator, as part of his AST role, delivering training in many primary and secondary schools across the south west; and
- the appointment of Year Achievement Co-ordinators to take the programme forward, releasing the Learning Co-ordinator to work 1:1 with teachers.

In October 2001, 83 teaching staff were surveyed about the value of the Learning Co-ordinator's role and the impact of new ideas about teaching and learning on their professional practice. The following results from 62 per cent of the staff indicated that:

- 68 per cent of staff thought that brain-based learning played a 'quite large' or 'large' role in planning their lessons;
- 56 per cent of staff found the role of the Learning Co-ordinator useful in providing resources and support; and
- 32 per cent of staff were regularly involved in Camborne School Learning Forum activities.

Conclusions

The mentored cohort of pupils at risk of underachieving was more than 10 per cent better than it would have been if they had not received 1:1 support. GCSE results are better in areas of the school where teachers actively think about pedagogy.

Despite these advantages it is important to highlight the limitations of the research. It is never easy in educational research to identify strict cause and effect relationships between interventions and outcomes due to the complexity of what takes place in the classroom. The professional enquiry approach used in the 'learning to learn' project presents further difficulties.

For example, the teachers involved in developing the learning approach are not necessarily best placed to evaluate its success, not only because of the demands on their time to do their job, but also because of their potential subjectivity. Of course, the Research Leader has attempted to ensure that this has not been the case by requesting a range of data from the schools, including results from national tests and testimony from colleagues. Many of the schools also identified control and comparison groups of pupils to assess the differential impact of the 'learning to learn' approaches, while others with actual results in national tests compared to predicted results.

Another risk with school-based research is that the findings cannot be generalized to other settings. This is partly because no two schools are the same, but also because the project schools were researching different approaches and aspects of 'learning to learn' with different age groups. This makes cross case analysis of the findings from the schools more problematic and is why the findings in Chapter 6 are presented with the names of the particular schools associated with each, as a way of showing that a 'learning to learn' approach will not necessarily produce all the results listed.

Despite these issues, we believe that the advantages of the research approach have far outweighed the limitations, not least because the teachers themselves have become skilled in research techniques and many have completed post-graduate qualifications as a result. We will be using a similar approach in Phase 3 of the research, working with a larger number of schools and supported by the University of Newcastle research team.

Support for the schools

Throughout the project the schools were provided with practical tools and resources as well as high-quality professional development. These included:

- ongoing individual consultation via telephone and email;
- visits from Jill Rodd;
- regular newsletters and an email discussion group;
- access to free resources such as CHAMPS, an online 'learning to learn' programme developed by Accelerated Learning Systems;
- pro-forma research tools, such as the indicators of success;
- termly professional development days which included external speakers, best practice workshops, and research support and guidance from Jill Rodd;
- three annual residential workshops which provided opportunities to meet as a group to plan, hear from external experts, share good practice and reflect on experiences and findings, and
- free places at the three National Conferences run to publicize the project and disseminate the findings.

During the course of Phase 1 all schools were offered at least one visit from an allocated Mentor, who was a member of the project Advisory Board or the Campaign's senior management team. Mentors were intended as critical friends for the schools; however, relatively few of the schools took up this opportunity. Therefore in Phase 2, Ray Wicks was seconded from Lloyds TSB as the project's Schools Liaison Officer. He visited all the project schools as a way of sharing practice and supporting their research.

Collecting the evidence

As a baseline for the project, MORI was commissioned by the Campaign to survey over 2000 11–16-year-old pupils in February 2000 and again in February 2002 on a range of 'learning to learn' issues. Some of the results are included on page 10, while the full results from the 2000 survey are included in *Learning to learn: setting the agenda for schools in the 21st century.*

As described above, as a way of measuring the impact of the different approaches across the schools in Phase 1, a standard questionnaire was administered at the beginning and end of the school year. A majority of the schools also identified target and comparison groups in order to evaluate the impact of their 'learning to learn' interventions.

Beyond this, individual schools decided what data were available and meaningful in terms of their specific project and school agenda. This included quantitative data, such as SAT and GCSE scores, reading and spelling ages, value added data, pre- and post-academic test scores, attitudinal and learning style surveys and attendance and exclusion and behaviour figures. Qualitative data was also collected, including Ofsted reports, pupil interviews, reflections in diaries and video-taped discussions.

The range of data collected was intended to provide evidence relating to:

- changes in pupils' performance, attainment and motivation,
- changes in pupils' understanding, attributes and attitudes,
- changes in teachers' practice and effectiveness, and
- changes in parental and wider community involvement (where relevant).

The participating teachers were given a standard format to guide the reporting of their findings. Many of them also wrote up their research for other audiences and objectives, such as reports to school governors, post-graduate qualifications, Best Practice Research scholarships and professional publications, and this provided additional information for the project.

What did the schools actually do?

Chapters 3 and 6 give many specific examples of what individual schools did to develop 'learning to learn', while the case studies through this book and in *Teaching pupils how to learn* and the Phase 2 Research Report give further examples. This section summarizes all the approaches adopted in Phases 1 and 2 into generic categories. The categories are not exclusive and many of the project schools adopted more than one of the approaches listed.

Stand alone 'learning to learn' courses

Several schools evaluated the impact of providing 'learning to learn' induction courses or ongoing timetabled lessons for pupils to explore how we learn and how they could 'learn to learn'. The content of these courses varied but all focused on developing some or all aspects of the 5 Rs for lifelong learning[1].

Using models of learning

Several schools assessed the impact of using different models of learning for planning and delivering lessons and of helping pupils develop their own models of learning.

Developing self-esteem, confidence and motivation

Several schools assessed different approaches to developing readiness, self-esteem, confidence and motivation through strategies such as Assessment for Learning, Accelerated Learning, Gestalt theory, peer teaching and NLP.

Learning styles

A number of schools monitored the emergence of preferred learning styles and/or helped pupils identify their preferred learning style and monitored the impact on independent learning. Several schools assessed how VAK approaches could improve pupil communication.

Multiple intelligences

A number of schools explored how multiple intelligences teaching and learning approaches could help raise standards and develop learnacy. Some schools also explored how Emotional Intelligence could be developed, for example through Quality Circle Time.

'Learning to learn' approaches embedded in specific curriculum areas

Some schools explored the application of Thinking Skills and 'learning to learn' approaches in specific subject areas (for example, CASE, CAME, Thinking through Geography).

'Learning to learn' approaches with specific groups of pupils (for example, gifted and talented, gender, disaffected learners, and so on)

One school identified specific target and control groups of gifted and talented pupils and monitored the effect of applying 'learning to learn' teaching and learning approaches. Another school assessed the impact of providing intensive mentoring support for disaffected pupils by mentors trained in NLP/'Learning to learn' approaches. Several schools assessed the differential impact of 'learning to learn' on different genders.

Pupils' learning strategies

A number of schools assessed the impact of developing Resourcefulness through giving pupils a toolkit of 'learning to learn' techniques, such as mind mapping techniques and NLP, and so on.

Teaching and learning approaches

Many of the schools evaluated the effectiveness of different 'learning to learn' teaching strategies such as delivering information through visual, auditory and kinesthetic approaches, following a learning cycle in all planning frameworks and/or teaching to meet the needs of different intelligences.

[1] *The Key Stage 3 learning toolkit* by Jackie Beere of Campaign School, and *Learning to learn: making learning work for all students* by Gary Burnett of Market Lambert School contain more detail of the courses in each of these secondary schools. See Resources section for details.

Learning environments

Some schools identified the impact of different aspects of a learning-friendly environment such as creating low threat, high-challenge learning opportunities, the use of ICT, interactive whiteboards and music in different curriculum areas, and the use of posters with learning messages and other visual stimulus as part of classroom display.

The body and learning

Several schools explored the impact of giving pupils information about how nutrition, water and sleep affect learning and/or provided brain-friendly food in school and access to water in the classroom. Several schools looked at the impact of Brain Gym®, yoga, meditation and other relaxation techniques on learning and exam results. One school explored the impact of an American Football course on motivation and concentration among disaffected boys.

Memory and reflection

Some schools explored the impact of different 'learning to learn' approaches on memory and recall and how this affected exam success. Most schools used different approaches to develop pupils' ability to reflect on and improve learning.

Teacher development and 'learning to learn' transfer

Most schools assessed the impact of engaging other staff in supporting 'learning to learn' approaches for example, through professional development and the production of resources/staff handbooks, and so on. Some schools explored how pupils could be helped to transfer and apply 'learning to learn' approaches in different contexts.

Involvement of parents and the wider community

Some schools assessed the impact of running courses, holding information evenings and producing resources for parents about 'learning to learn', including the impact on parental perceptions of the school.

Wider learning and school culture

Many of the schools investigated aspects of developing a wider school culture to support 'learning to learn', for example through changes to the School Development Plan, curriculum, use of assemblies, citizenship learning and out-of-school hours learning.

What will Phase 3 of the 'learning to learn' project involve?

The Campaign for Learning is now developing a larger research project (Phase 3) which will build on and develop the findings to date. We will be working with clusters of up to 12 schools in:

- Cheshire LEA
- Enfield EAZ
- Cornwall EAZ

A team led by Steve Higgins at the University of Newcastle Thinking Skills Research Centre will provide the research support for the project.

As in Phases 1 and 2, the rationale for the project will be to understand how we can help pupils to learn most effectively and so give each one the best chance to achieve his or her full potential.

Specifically, the research will aim to understand:

- the relative importance of different 'learning to learn' approaches in raising standards;
- how the adoption of 'learning to learn' approaches impacts on teacher motivation and capacity to manage change;
- whether, and if so how, 'learning to learn' approaches support the development of confident and capable lifelong learners.

The project will run in schools for three years from September 2003 and will use the 5 Rs for lifelong learning framework for structuring the research.

Conclusion

The 'learning to learn' project has made a significant start in identifying how and in what ways a 'learning to learn' approach can make a difference in schools. At the same time, the process of conducting the research itself has been hugely developmental for the teachers and schools involved. However, it would be wrong to suggest that the project has not had its challenges, and these are set out in detail in the project's second research report. Issues have centred on the difficulties of communicating with schools and on the lack of capacity within some schools to research and reflect on teaching and learning in this focused way.

5 | The research findings

This chapter summarizes the key findings from Phase 2 (September 2001 to July 2002) of the 'learning to learn' school-based professional enquiry. The full findings from Phases 1 and 2 are included in the respective project research reports available on the Campaign's website www.campaign-for-learning.org.uk.

It is important to note that the findings from the project remain indicative at this stage. A number of the challenges involved in conducting school-based professional enquiry were referred to in the last chapter and these are discussed in more detail in the Phase 1 Project research report. It is partly in order to confirm and deepen the findings with a larger sample of schools over a longer time period that the Campaign has embarked on the next three-year phase of the 'learning to learn' project in partnership with the University of Newcastle's Thinking Skills Research Centre.

The summary of Phase 2 research findings is organized under the following headings:

- the learner
- the learning process
- the learning environment
- the teacher
- the body.

At the end of this chapter a number of the implications of the key findings for current educational priorities as well as a set of recommendations for policy that emerge from the research findings are drawn out.

Summary of the Phase 2 research findings

These findings have been organized into sections relating to the main stems of the mind map on page 45, which was used as a framework to plan the Phase 2 research with schools. The main sources of evidence for each finding are listed according to which school they came from.

There is insufficient space in this publication to report in detail the data collected that relates to each particular finding, although the case studies included throughout the book provide examples of the types of evidence they are drawn from. Detailed descriptions and data for each school are available in the Phase 2 project research report.

The findings have been produced on photocopiable pages for ease of use in teacher professional development activities.

Research findings

The learner

Summary: There are positive effects on standards and motivation of pupils who understand their preferred learning style, their multiple/emotional intelligence and Hermann Brain Dominance profiles, and the 5 Rs for lifelong learning.

❏ Students of all ages are more positive about learning and motivated to learn when they understand their preferred learning styles and intelligences (evidence from Campion, Cornwallis, Cramlington, Ellowes Hall, Hipsburn, Kingdown, Ogmore, Prince William, West Grove).

❏ Learners with a sensory preference for taking in information kinesthetically experience greater success where teachers deliver information using the full range of sensory modalities (evidence from Ashgate, Campion, Hipsburn, Ladysmith, Kingdown, Prince William).

❏ Encouraging the development of pupils' learning dispositions, including the 5 Rs of Readiness, Resourcefulness, Resilience, Remembering and Reflectiveness enhances pupils' perceptions of themselves as learners and improves attainment levels (evidence from Christchurch, Ellowes Hall, Hipsburn, Ladysmith, Summerhill, West Grove).

❏ Pupils learn best when they enjoy themselves or have fun, indicating that their emotional state is fundamental to learning (evidence from Cornwallis, Hipsburn, Ogmore, Prince William).

❏ One-to-one mentoring with a mentor who is trained in 'learning to learn' approaches is highly effective with underachieving boys and girls for improving examination results. The content of the mentoring is more effective for boys if it is differentiated to place more emphasis on flexibility, breaking tasks into small steps, greater use of ICT, more frequent contact with parents and practical support (evidence from Camborne).

❏ A small number of traditionally academic pupils thought that teaching about learning styles and multiple intelligences was a waste of time and that this time should be devoted to subject areas (evidence from Prince William).

Research findings

The learning process

Summary: There are positive effects on pupils' standards and motivation where pupils understand models of brain-friendly, student-centred learning; appreciate the importance of self-esteem and motivation in learning; are able to identify and apply a range of strategies; and have their age and the time of day taken into account by teachers responsible for planning learning.

❑ Foundation Stage and Key Stage 1 and 2 pupils demonstrate increased enjoyment of and improved learning when they understand how they learn best and have a range of learning tools to apply to different tasks (evidence from Hipsburn, Ladysmith, West Grove).

❑ Discussion about learning helps pupils of all ages to become more metacognitive (evidence from Hipsburn, Ladysmith, Prince William).

❑ 'Learning to learn' courses help primary and secondary students identify and apply a range of strategies that they think help them learn at school and at home. The techniques that are considered to be useful and used by students include Brain Gym®, mind mapping, memory techniques, posters and diagrams, interactive whiteboards and working with peers (evidence from Camborne, Campion, Cornwallis, Cramlington, Ellowes Hall, Hipsburn, Ladysmith, Ogmore, Prince William, Sandwich).

❑ The vast majority of secondary students enjoy and value taking part in 'learning to learn' sessions and courses. They think 'learning to learn' courses are worthwhile, that what they learn helps with other schoolwork and that they should be part of the regular school timetable (evidence from Camborne, Cornwallis, Cramlington, Ellowes Hall, Kingdown, Ogmore, Prince William).

❑ Where 'learning to learn' is offered to secondary students outside the usual timetable, improved student motivation, productivity and independent learning is evident (evidence from Campion, Kingdown).

continued...

The learning process (cont.)

❏ Secondary students can transfer the strategies learned in 'learning to learn' courses to other areas of the curriculum provided teachers in those curriculum areas are given professional development and reference 'learning to learn' approaches (evidence from Cramlington, Campion, Ogmore).

❏ Parents who understand about 'learning to learn' approaches feel more confident about trying different ways to help their children learn at home (evidence from Hipsburn, Malet Lambert).

Research findings

The learning environment

Summary: There are positive effects on the standards and motivation of pupils associated with the location of learning; the physical environment for learning (including the use of displays, pictures and music); learning tools used (including the use of ICT and interactive whiteboards); and where pupil groupings are taken into consideration in planning for learning.

❑ Attractive physical learning environments are associated with improved pupil attitudes, behaviour and performance (evidence from Ellowes Hall, Hipsburn, Kingdown, Ogmore).

❑ Posters, pictures and displays provide pupils with a structure through which to recognize, select and reinforce learning behaviours (evidence from Cramlington, Hipsburn, Ellowes Hall, Kingdown, Ladysmith).

❑ The use of music as a tool for learning improves standards and motivation in secondary students (evidence from Ogmore).

❑ Boys' learning in particular is enhanced by opportunities to use ICT (evidence from Camborne, Ellowes Hall).

Ogmore School

South Wales, 11–18 Mixed Comprehensive

Research area

The development of a 'Music for Learning' strategy

Hypotheses

Different pieces of music are linked to different styles of teaching and support.

Pupil standards can be raised by using music as a tool for learning in subjects across the curriculum.

Pupil motivation is affected by the use of music in the classroom.

There are differences between the ways that different pupils respond to music in lessons.

Research focus

A range of teachers and subject areas including mathematics, science, history, Welsh, English and business studies

Target group and Comparison group of pupils in Year 8 (science) and Year 11 (English)

Teachers of and pupils studying mathematics (Test and Control Groups in Year 8)

Methodology

Following meetings about the use of music in lessons in order to raise standards and a pilot study of one teacher's music lessons and the ways pupils responded physically and mentally to different pieces of music, a catalogue of music was created entitled 'Music & the Mind Learning Collection'. This is a musical collection of five different catalogues each with different purposes for teachers to use during lessons, break times, assemblies and registration periods. The purposes of the five catalogues include:

- ■ to promote the learning of specific information and skills;
- ■ to relax and calme;
- ■ to motivate, stimulate and energize;
- ■ to faciliate specific tasks, such as brain storming, meditation, group work, individual task, reflection, evaluation of work.

Teachers were given the extracts of music and guidelines on when and how to use them.

Data collected included:

- teachers' verbal responses in interviews
- teachers' questionnaires
- individual pupil diaries
- pupil interviews
- pupil questionnaires.

Success criteria

Raised standards

Increased motivation

Teaching styles and support vary according to music chosen

Key findings

All of the teachers (100 per cent) and the vast majority of pupils who took part in the research responded with very positive attitudes to the use of music in lessons.

The use of Music & the Mind supported both teachers and pupils.

Boys and girls respond differently to music in different lessons and situations and not all boys and girls respond to music the same way.

Teachers' preference for a piece of music influenced their choice and consequently some overuse of certain pieces had an adverse effect on some pupils.

Data from the teachers revealed the following findings:

- 100 per cent enjoyed using music in their lessons.
- 100 per cent thought that music supported them and helped them to relax during lessons.
- 65 per cent thought that it stopped them from raising their voice towards pupils, especially the relaxation and calming music.
- 100 per cent thought that pupils settled better at the beginning of lessons.
- 91 per cent thought that pupils had improved their study skills.
- 66 per cent thought that pupils had achieved better grades.
- 75 per cent thought that pupils retained better concentration during lessons.
- 100 per cent would like more catalogues of music.
- 78 per cent would like a wider range of music to support their teaching.
- 94 per cent thought that using music in their classrooms made the experience of teaching far more enjoyable.
- 100 per cent wanted to continue their involvement in the use of Music & the Mind.

Specifically data from the pupils indicated that during the time when the music was played:

■ 100 per cent felt like working.

■ 81 per cent concentrated all the time.

■ 76 per cent felt happy.

■ 92 per cent were more relaxed.

■ 69 per cent thought that they achieved 'quite a lot'.

■ 92 per cent thought that it helped them with their studying and concentration skills.

■ Under 7 per cent of pupils reported negative comments about music played in lessons.

Conclusions

When music is used in a constructive way in lessons, the response is positive. Pupils' evidence suggests that learning with the aid of music does motivate them better and helps them concentrate when developing study skills. It had a positive effect on calming the pupils, accelerated learning and the application of self-study skills. However, pupils' ability to reflect on their learning and comment on their performance needs to be developed. There is some evidence to suggest that the use of music raised standards. Teachers need further support in using music to measure learning.

Creating a learning to learn school - *research and practice for raising standards, motivation and morale*

Research findings

The teacher

Summary: Being involved in 'learning to learn' has significant benefits in relation to teacher motivation; participation in ongoing continuing professional development; the roles and work of other adults in and out of the classroom (for example, parents and teaching assistants) and for effective mentoring of both pupils and colleagues.

❏ Improved pupil performance in examinations is associated with teachers who actively think about teaching and learning issues (evidence from Camborne, Ellowes Hall, Hipsburn).

❏ Student learning and behaviour is improved when teachers employ 'learning to learn' teaching strategies (evidence from Campion, Ellowes Hall, Hipsburn, Kingdown, Ogmore, Prince William, West Grove).

❏ Teachers' motivation and enjoyment is increased when they adopt 'learning to learn' approaches (evidence from Campion, Ellowes Hall, Hipsburn, Ladysmith, Ogmore, Summerhill, West Grove).

❏ Pupils are happier and perform better where they have teachers who embrace 'learning to learn' dispositions themselves, such as being flexible, open-minded, willing to experiment and embrace change (evidence from Camborne, Hipsburn, West Grove).

❏ Active resistance by teachers and departments to 'learning to learn' is related to pupil performance that is significantly below average (evidence from Camborne).

❏ 'Learning to learn' approaches can help to create a school ethos and culture where learning is valued by all (evidence from Camborne, Cornwallis, Hipsburn, West Grove).

❏ 'Learning to learn' helps motivate teachers to undertake and actively engage in a range of professional development activities (evidence from Camborne, Cramlington, Hipsburn, Ladysmith, Ogmore, Summerhill).

❏ Parents who participate in a 'learning to learn' course become more effective in supporting their children's learning and become better learners themselves (evidence from Hipsburn, Malet Lambert).

The body

Summary: There are positive effects on standards and motivation of pupils related to hydration (that is water available in classrooms); information about the importance of nutrition and sleep for learning; and the use of exercise and relaxation techniques.

- ❏ Pupils learn better if they have free access to drinking water (evidence from Hipsburn, Ladysmith, Prince William, Summerhill).

- ❏ Exercise in the form of Brain Gym® and sport has a positive effect on pupil enjoyment of and motivation for learning (evidence from Hipsburn, Prince William).

- ❏ The use of music in classrooms has a positive effect on calming and relaxing pupils (evidence from Hipsburn, Ogmore).

- ❏ Engaging in specific de-stressing activities before written examinations improves pupils' examination results (evidence from Prince William).

Implications of the key findings for current educational priorities

Chapter 2 sets out the current policy context for schools and draws out some of the implications of 'learning to learn' for how policy might change in the future. This section takes some of the specific issues that currently concern the government, researchers, schools and the media and highlights findings from the project that have relevance for these debates.

Gender differences

● Boys' learning appears to be enhanced when the content of 'learning to learn' approaches are differentiated to take into account their interests and needs (evidence from Ashgate, Camborne).

Independent learning

● Pupils who undertake a 'learning to learn' course show evidence of a strong sense of responsibility for their own learning (evidence from Ellowes Hall, Hipsburn).

Key Stage 3 dip in learning

● The overwhelmingly positive response by Year 7 pupils to 'learning to learn' approaches suggests that they may be practical and useful strategies for addressing concerns about negative pupil attitudes to learning as they move towards Year 8 (evidence from Campion, Ellowes Hall, Ogmore, Sandwich).

Kinesthetic learning

● Building in kinesthetic learning opportunities appears to improve pupils' motivation (evidence from Ashgate, Campion, Hipsburn, Kingdown, Ladysmith, Prince William).

● Disaffected learners with a preference for taking in information kinesthetically experience greater levels of success and improved chances of going to university where teachers teach according to their preferred learning style (evidence from Campion).

● Learners with a preference for taking in information kinesthetically who participate in a sporting workshop focused on raising achievement display improved attitudes to learning and raised performance (evidence from Prince William).

Parental involvement in learning

● Offering 'learning to learn' sessions and courses to parents encourages them to become involved in and support their children's learning at home and at school (evidence from Camborne, Hipsburn, Malet Lambert, Prince William).

● Parents increasingly value learning and gain in confidence as co-educators where they have participated in a 'learning to learn' course (evidence from Hipsburn, Malet Lambert).

Parental perceptions of schools

● Recruitment and retention are not issues in schools where 'learning to learn' is embedded (evidence from West Grove).

● Parents express a high degree of satisfaction for schools that embed 'learning to learn' throughout the school (evidence from Hipsburn, Malet Lambert, West Grove).

School leadership and management

- 'Learning to learn' is most effective for pupils and teachers where there is high-profile leadership from the head and SMT and where it is embedded in whole school planning from department level to the School Development Plan (evidence from Camborne, Ellowes Hall, Hipsburn, Ladysmith, Kingdown, West Grove).
- Where 'learning to learn' is implemented as a whole-school approach, all teachers and teaching assistants take responsibility for curriculum development and for leading others (evidence from Hipsburn, Ladysmith, West Grove).

School workforce and teacher motivation

- Teachers' motivation and enjoyment is increased when they adopt 'learning to learn' approaches (evidence from Campion, Ellowes Hall, Hipsburn, Ladysmith, Ogmore, Summerhill, West Grove).
- 'Learning to learn' motivates teachers to undertake and actively engage in a range of professional development activities (evidence from Camborne, Cramlington, Hipsburn, Ladysmith, Ogmore, Summerhill).
- Working at a school that adopts 'learning to learn' approaches improves confidence as a professional in teaching assistants and other adults in the classroom (evidence from Hipsburn).

Social inclusion

- A one-to-one mentoring programme did not work effectively for meeting the learning and self-esteem needs of pupils who have firmly adopted life styles and values that involve drug use with parental consent, non-attendance with parental support and who receive minimal support from home (evidence from Camborne).

Underachievement/pupils at risk of disaffection

- Teaching Year 11 pupils on the C/D borderline about multiple intelligences enhances self-esteem, self-belief and motivation, thereby opening access to achievement, (evidence from Prince William).

case
study

Malet Lambert School

Hull, 11–18 Mixed Comprehensive

Research area

A twelve-session 'learning to learn' course ('Parents and Children Working Together') for parents of secondary school students

Hypothesis

Parents who undertake an accredited 'learning to learn' course will become more effective in supporting their children with learning and will become better learners themselves.

Research focus

Ten parents of secondary school students

Methodology

The course for parents built on the Phase 1 work where ideas and strategies for learning were developed in the 'learning to learn' course for students. It was delivered over 12 evenings in two and a half hour sessions and was developed by a teacher at the school in collaboration with a lecturer from the University of Lincolnshire and Humberside (UHL). The course was taught in two parts and covered topics on learning styles, multiple intelligences, communication skills, improving learning performance and action planning as well as introducing the parents to selected ICT skills and resources such as working with Windows, word processing, email, internet and CD ROMs. An optional visit to ULH's Virtual Campus was offered to the parents.

The course was offered for accreditation at ULH where it was awarded the credit status of six points. The ten parents who took part received a certificate of completion from the University at an awards ceremony.

It was evaluated using qualitative data from parent questionnaires and a video debate, which was transcribed for detailed qualitative analysis.

Success criteria

Parental use of the qualification with other children, for example, as a paid learning mentor or teacher's aide or in a voluntary capacity.

Deeper understanding among parents about the learning process.

Increased parental confidence to help their children to learn.

More active involvement by parents in promoting effective learning in their children.

More active involvement of parents in the school, as learners, helpers and participants in learning events, for example, school trips, revision evenings, parent support groups.

Key findings

Qualitative data from the parent questionnaires indicated that parents:

- undertook the course because they thought that it would be of benefit not only to their children but also to themselves in their relationships with their children. The computer skills were considered to help them in their work.

- felt uncomfortable about being out in the spotlight and playing games and some were concerned by their inadequate computer skills.

- appreciated the general presentation style and warm atmosphere, the handouts, the focus on children and the brain, looking at different software and the encouragement of optimistic and positive attitude to learning.

- thought that the benefits as parents included insight into how to help their children, the importance of being patient, and being more informed and confident about what they are doing with their children.

- thought that the benefits included greater personal confidence in everyday life and at work and understanding of themselves as a learner.

- have adapted and used what they learned in their work and with their children.

- have changed the way they listen to and encourage their children, taken control to pursue the things they want in life and at work, gained confidence and made constructive plans for improving aspects of home life and work.

Overall, the parents were very positive about the course and its benefits.

Analysis of the transcript of the video debate indicated that the parents found the course to be valuable, from parental comments such as:

- 'the learning culture at home has changed...I've tried to open my children's minds to think that anything is possible'.

- 'to help your child, we have got the knowledge now to say 'well, have you tried this approach?' Have you tried this in the classroom, does that work and you can ask more questions like that rather than just saying "oh well, if he can't do it, then he can't do it". '

- 'I think if you could sum 'learning to learn' up in one word, for me it is self-belief and for the children as well'.

- 'the children need this course now, or even at Year 5, so that they can have the foundations there already for the Year 6 onslaught'.

- 'surely education officials must know in the back of their minds that after all of their supposed experience that maths, science, times tables is not the only way forward, it's learning how you are actually, because they are intelligent people and I know they are mixed up with statistics and targets'.

It is anticipated that part of the course will be offered on-line and developed as a distance learning package that includes multimedia materials.

Conclusions

Parents who understand about 'learning to learn' approaches developed more self-confidence in their daily and working lives and felt more confident about trying different ways to help their children learn at home.

The parents valued the incorporation of 'learning to learn' into their children's education from the earliest stages and thought that it would help children cope with certain stresses, for example, assessment tests and transition to secondary school.

They believed that teachers would benefit from learning about and implementing these approaches and that this would take a lot of tension out of the relationship between teachers, children and parents and make the classroom a happier place to be.

The parents were more confident to become actively involved in aspects of school life, home life and their work.

Creating a learning to learn school - *research and practice for raising standards, motivation and morale*

Recommendations for policy emerging from the research findings

Clear evidence has been assembled in the two years of this project that signpost a number of key messages and recommendations for improving teaching and learning.

- 'Learning to learn' has a positive impact on pupil standards and motivation. Teachers should be encouraged and supported with time (curriculum and non-contact) and resources to apply 'learning to learn' principles and practices with pupils of all ages. Teachers should be helped to use 'learning to learn' principles and practices in terms of how they structure the learning environment, deliver information, facilitate learning opportunities, use new technologies and provide formative feedback.

- 'Learning to learn' helps develop positive knowledge, skills and attitudes for pupils' independent and lifelong learning. Further work should be undertaken by the DfES to support schools to focus on developing these qualities as a priority, including through changes to the curriculum where necessary. Schools and Local Education Authorities should offer 'learning to learn' opportunities to children, parents and other members of the local community.

- 'Learning to learn' has a positive impact on teacher morale and motivation. Greater professional understanding and skills in 'learning to learn' will create more competent and confident teachers. The inclusion of 'learning to learn' modules and opportunities for teacher research in initial and ongoing teacher training and development offers a positive strategy for addressing the current retention problem. Therefore, DfES and its agencies should ensure that 'learning to learn' thinking and practice is included in initial teacher training and continuing professional development for teachers and support staff, including through an enhanced programme of teacher-led research.

- The role of the headteacher and senior management in actively leading and supporting the development of 'learning to learn' approaches and a learning culture in the school are critical. Schools should develop whole-school cross-curricula approaches which emphasize the value of learning both in and out of the classroom and through which pupils learn to apply 'learning to learn' in all areas.

- 'Learning to learn' has a positive impact on parents' support of and involvement with their children's learning. Schools and Local Education Authorities should offer parents a range of opportunities to understand the process of learning and themselves as learners so that they can effectively support their children's learning. Informed parents are more likely to work in partnership with teachers to support their children. Equally, broader community and family learning opportunities conducted in schools can help develop positive attitudes and skills related to lifelong learning as well as increased commitment to and involvement in school activities.

- 'Learning to learn' provides a focus for the development of a culture of inquiry and a community of researchers within a school. DfES should support the development of 'learning to learn' specialist schools as a means of furthering our understanding in this area and spreading good practice. Individual schools should embed 'learning to learn' through policies and in development plans so that it is integrated with other initiatives. This will encourage teachers, support staff and pupils to adopt a proactive role in shaping systems of practice, exchange and collaboration.

- The emerging evidence about the impact of 'learning to learn' on standards and motivation requires further research and validation. Further funded research that brings together teachers, academics, researchers and policy makers should be conducted with a wider sample of representative schools, especially in relation to the impact of 'learning to learn' on current educational priorities.

6 | Making it happen: how you can develop 'learning to learn' in your school

Teachers flourish best when, in key stage teams or departments (or more rarely whole schools), their talk is predominantly about teaching and learning and where, unconnected with appraisal, they are privileged to observe each other teach; to plan and review their work together; and to practise the habit of learning from each other new teaching techniques. But how does this state of affairs arise?

Professor Tim Brighouse, Foreword, Leading the Learning School

Chapter 3 set out what 'learning to learn' actually involves and drew out many of the key practical implications of this at the level of the classroom. This chapter looks more widely at how 'learning to learn' can be developed, implemented and supported at the level of the school.

At the heart of this section is the question 'What do you want your "learning to learn" approach to be?' It does not attempt to provide a blueprint for action or to suggest that there is a 'right' way to develop 'learning to learn', since every school and teacher is different and has a different set of influences and priorities. Instead, this chapter tries to give some structure to your own thinking and includes practical 'development activities' and resources you can use with colleagues to structure your thinking and discussions as you develop an approach.

Given the research finding in the last chapter that 'learning to learn' approaches work best with active support from the head and SMT of schools, this chapter starts with a brief overview of thinking about Learning Centred, or Instructional, Leadership. This leadership approach is widely accepted as the most effective model for successful school leadership and involves all staff in taking responsibility for improving teaching and learning within the school. It is included here because the approach is highly complementary to 'learning to learn', as the headteachers of the project schools throughout the chapter indicate.

The chapter then goes on to consider how some of the project schools have actually implemented 'learning to learn' approaches. It structures their approach using some of the key questions that you will need to answer in developing a distinctive 'learning to learn' approach for your school or classroom:

- Where are you starting from?
- How could 'learning to learn' fit with other initiatives already in place?
- Where do you want to get to?
- How will you implement the approach?

Learning centred leadership

Chapter 2 summarized some of the key developments in national education policy and in particular the current emphasis on developing school leadership through the Leadership Incentive Grant and the National College for School Leadership (NCSL). This section highlights some of the thinking about Learning Centred, or Instructional, Leadership now being promoted by the NCSL.

The Ten Propositions for School Leadership that underpin the Learning Centred Leadership model are set out in the box below. It is interesting how strongly the approach resonates with 'learning to learn' in its focus on developing a learning community of staff with an interest in teaching and learning issues. 'Learning Centred Leadership has, at its heart, a focus on learning', states the NCSL's Leading Edge development programme. 'It is about developing learning and teaching schools where there is a shared language to talk about pedagogical issues and a consistent, unifying emphasis on improving learning for all.'

The Ten School Leadership Propositions

School leaders must:

- be purposeful, inclusive and values driven;
- embrace the distinctive and inclusive context of the school;
- promote an active view of learning;
- be instructionally focused;
- be a function that is distributed throughout the school;
- build capacity by developing the school as a learning community;
- be futures orientated and strategically driven;
- be developed through experiential and innovative methodologies;
- be served by a support and policy context that is coherent and implementation driven; and
- be supported by a National College that leads the discourse around leadership for learning.

The research that has informed the model shows that effective school leaders all have the ability to define and communicate a coherent set of objectives with a map of how to reach them. As the lead learner of a learning community, the head actively tries to ensure that all staff actually adopt individualized and enquiry-based approaches to learning. This tends to include providing co-ordinated Continuing Professional Development (CPD) opportunities for teachers and other staff and undertaking CPD themselves as a context for open-minded, enquiry-based experimentation and debate with staff about which pedagogical strategies might best achieve the positive learning goals the school has for its pupils.

Such heads might also be expected to take a close interest in organizational issues relating to the learning that takes place in the classroom, such as the curriculum, timetable, composition of classes, the working patterns of teachers and the ways in which their 'free' time is used to promote collegiality and experimentation. Equally, such heads might actively seek to reach agreement with staff about, for example, what counts as a 'good lesson', what theories of learning are appropriate to the achievement of particular curricular objectives, and so on.

This kind of behaviour from heads means that thinking about teaching and learning have a high priority in ordinary conversation and formal discussion in school. 'Ideas about good teaching and effective learning are thus routinely shared, and people's success – both pupils' and teachers' – is continuously paraded and celebrated. This creates an ethos in which high standards are expected of everyone, and in which the virtues of hard work are esteemed' state the authors of a recent review of research and practice.

Where are you starting from?

Lesson plans should be the combined wisdom of a department, developed as a collective activity. Teachers should bring their creation to the table for others to look at, learn from, comment on and improve.

Derek Wise, Headteacher, Cramlington Community High School, Northumberland

In terms of your school's adoption of 'learning to learn' approaches, it could be that you feel you are a lone advocate, part of a small group in an otherwise sceptical atmosphere, or perhaps in a climate where such thinking and practice are the norm. Whatever your situation, an essential first step is to take stock of your school's and your own teaching and learning approach.

In addition to formal statements and documents you will have a sense of this from observing other teachers' lessons, through feedback from pupils or from the professional atmosphere in the staffroom. Equally, systematic auditing and feedback mechanisms may be in place within school to continually review and improve teaching and learning. If this is not the case you may find it useful to start the discussions with colleagues in your school by conducting new research into pupils' attitudes to learning, using questions along the lines of the MORI question that appears on page 10.

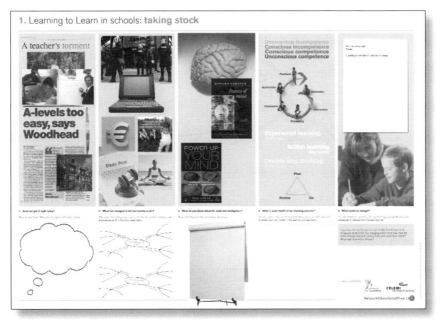

Once you have this kind of data, you could work with colleagues through the discussion mat included with *Teaching pupils how to learn* (additional copies of these are available in packs of ten from Network Educational Press – see Resources section). The mat uses pictures and eight different discussion scaffolds to help groups of teachers think about why and how they could develop a 'learning to learn' approach in their school. The following activity is adapted from the mat and draws on your own experience to assess what has changed in the wider world and schools over the past 20 years.

Professional development activity 1

With groups of up to six colleagues, discuss and agree what has changed in the past 20 years in the wider world and in schools. Use the key areas on the two mind maps below to structure your discussion and thinking and try to agree three key points for each area. Once you have completed the two maps, ask yourselves whether changes in schools have kept pace with changes in the wider world in a way that prepares children for that world.

What does a good 'learning to learn' school look like?

Another important auditing approach is to benchmark your school against what happens in other schools you know and what is more widely considered good practice. The NCSL's Leading Edge Development Programme for school leaders explores what three categories of school (Emergent, Established and Advanced) actually look like when they implement a Learning Centred Leadership approach. This provides a useful framework for schools to think about where they are starting from in developing their 'learning to learn' approach. Of course, both Learning Centred Leadership and 'learning to learn' must be implemented holistically at a number of levels, but it is worth drawing out here the following section from the Leading Edge programme materials, describing how such schools build their knowledge base to support effective teaching and learning.

Emergent	Established	Advanced
Staff attend courses. The TES appears in the staffroom. There are pockets of knowledge and informal sharing.	A professional collection is available to all staff and key articles are displayed, circulated or summarized. Knowledge is shared in a planned way and makes an impact. The school encourages further study.	The school expects and supports continuing adult learning as a key part of professionalism. Readings are studied and shared regularly (e.g. key point summaries and study groups). A high proportion of teaching and support staff are involved in progressive further study (e.g. MEd, MBA, DPhil, NCSL Research Associates).
Professional growth is enhanced through courses about teaching and learning which are shared within the school.	Initiatives such as performance management and IiP have been used to bring coherence to instructional development across the school. There are well-established arrangements for setting and reviewing objectives, induction, mentoring and progressive development of all staff in the organization.	Enquiry based teams and flexible professional partnerships generate new thinking about learning. This is modelled by the involvement of the headteacher as lead learner and by other members of the leadership team with key instructional roles (e.g. as a statement of values, all members of a secondary leadership team have been accredited as Advanced Skills Teachers).

Emergent	Established	Advanced
Teachers visit each other's classrooms informally.	There is a planned programme of focused visits, with outcomes shared, recorded and acted upon. School uses university and external expertise when required. Opportunities to share best practice.	A programme of practitioner enquiry includes intervisitation (e.g. visits to other partner schools, and Best Practice Research Scholarships, international visits or teacher exchanges). The school consistently and coherently reaches out to new thinking and practice through established partnerships (e.g. links with Open University staff, conferences/papers to celebrate and challenge practice).

From: *How does the school build its knowledge base about effective teaching and learning?*
Learning Centred Leadership, Leading Edge development course materials, NCSL)

How could 'learning to learn' fit with other initiatives already in place?

'Learning to learn's focus on the learner, the learning process and the development of lifelong learning attitudes, skills and knowledge clearly makes it an approach in its own right. But, as Chapter 3 described, there are many different approaches that can be adopted and adapted to contribute towards a 'learning to learn' approach in the school or classroom. One advantage of this is that every school will already have some elements of a potential 'learning to learn' approach in place. Given how stretched teachers are it is important to identify and build on these opening points, using them to demonstrate that embracing 'learning to learn' does not necessarily mean developing a whole new set of activities. 'Learning to learn' can and should be an evolution, not a revolution, in your school.

The list on the next page gives some examples of initiatives and approaches that your school may already be involved in. Use this as a simple auditing tool to assess what you can build from and what you might do next to bring together your 'learning to learn' approach.

Checklist of initiatives to audit existing 'learning to learn' approaches in school

Initiative	Already in development/place	Will develop as part of 'learning to learn'
● 14–19 pilots		
● Accelerated Learning initiatives e.g. ALPS (Alistair Smith), CHAMPS (www.learntolearn.org) and /or Critical Skills Programme		
● Artsmark		
● Assessment for Learning / Formative Assessment		
● Basic Skills Quality Mark		
● Beacon School		
● Building Learning Power/ Evaluating Lifelong Learning project (ELLI)		
● Circle Time		
● Citizenship		
● Creativity, including Creative Partnerships		
● Education Action Zone		
● Emotional Literacy programmes		
● Excellence in Cities		
● Extended Schools/Community Schools Network		
● Healthy Schools Programme		
● Investors in Excellence		
● Investors in People		
● IQEA (Improving the Quality of Education for All)		
● Key Stage 3 Strategy/Teaching and Learning in Foundation Subjects		
● Leadership Incentive Grant		
● National Literacy and Numeracy Strategies		
● National College for School Leadership		
● Networked Learning Communities/NCSL		
● Playing for Success		
● Pupil Learning Credits		
● RSA Opening Minds Research		
● Specialist/Advanced School		
● Sports Mark		
● Study Support Activities (after school clubs)		
● Sure Start Programme		
● The Classroom of the Future and ICT Initiatives, e.g. Curriculum Online		
● Thinking Skills Projects, including Cognitive Acceleration through Science Education (CASE), Cognitive Acceleration through Maths Education (CAME), Cognitive Acceleration through Technology Education (CATE), Somerset Thinking Skills Project, Philosophy for Children, Thinking through (Newcastle University TSRC), TOC, etc.		
● Tops Sports and Dance Programmes		
● University of the First Age (UFA)		

University of the First Age (UfA)

Where do you want to get to?

'Learning to learn' is embedded in our classroom culture. The 3 Rs are on display and specific 'learning to learn' objectives will form part of the shared learning objectives.

Neil Baker, Headteacher, Christ Church Primary School, Wiltshire

Close relationships exist between all stakeholders in our school, built on trust and mutual respect. Staff morale is high and I am always inundated with applications for new posts. Most importantly, the pupils are confident in themselves as learners.

Elaine Wilmot, Headteacher, West Grove Primary School, London

Having identified where you are starting from and what a good 'learning to learn' school looks like, then having audited the initiatives already in place that you could build on, the next step is to develop a clear vision of where you want to get to. You may want to use the school's School Development Plan or other existing work as a starting point. Or you could use the mind map activity on page 116, but this time agree what you want the different areas to look and feel like in five, ten or 20 years' time.

The important thing is to have a clear sense of what you want to see, hear and feel as you walk through your own classroom of the future. The quotes at the start of this section might help, as might the following Teaching and Learning Statement and Strategy from West Grove Primary School, practical examples and ideas.

WEST GROVE PRIMARY SCHOOL
TEACHING AND LEARNING POLICY

Revised Summer 2000

RATIONALE

To formulate a policy, which promotes achievement in our school, by stating an entitlement, for all pupils, to a broad and balanced curriculum, which will provide opportunities for them to develop their full potential.

AIMS

1. To improve the quality of teaching and learning experiences offered to pupils.

2. To clarify current practice and determine future approaches to teaching and learning.

3. To convey our basic philosophy about Teaching and Learning.

4. To provide an agreed framework which underpins all areas of the curriculum.

The policy identifies the common processes of learning which inform and guide our teaching.

REVIEW, MONITORING AND EVALUATION

Quality teaching and learning will be the focus of classroom monitoring.

Senior Managers will undertake monitoring in the school and findings reported to whole staff at staff meetings. The Policy will be modified, as necessary, following discussion with staff and will be presented for ratification by the Governors.

Standards of achievement will be monitored by staff and governors and the Teaching and Learning Policy evaluated in the light of statistical evidence, as necessary.

WEST GROVE PRIMARY SCHOOL
TEACHING AND LEARNING POLICY

CHARACTERISTICS OF GOOD TEACHING AND LEARNING AT WEST GROVE PRIMARY SCHOOL

TEACHING

Learning will be facilitated by the progressive acquisition of knowledge, skills and understanding and by:

1. Using teaching techniques that make use of appropriate methods suiting the topic or subject as well as the pupils' stage of development and preferred learning styles.

2. Lessons having clear aims and purposes as indicated in our planning which takes into account Early Learning Goals, Attainment Targets and Programmes of Study of the National Curriculum.

3. Teachers having high expectations of each pupils in all areas of the curriculum.

4. Accentuating the positive in behaviour, work and attitude and by setting a good example.

5. Children being involved in varying degrees with planning, organising and evaluating their own learning, e.g. they should receive regular feedback to help them progress through thoughtful marking and discussion.

6. Ensuring that relationships are positive and promote pupil motivation by making pupils feel welcomed, cared for, secure and valued as individuals, by developing their self-esteem and confidence. We do this through building on strengths to promote success, regular meetings with children and parents and by using our system of rewards.

7. Where appropriate, children being given work to do at home, which may be: spellings, tables, reading activities or work which complements and extends the work done in lessons. We encourage parents to help children with their learning at home.

8. Encouraging children to show concern for others and to value each person's individual contribution.

9. Providing as many opportunities as possible for first hand experience and investigative work.

10. Flexible teaching strategies; children should have the opportunity to be taught in whole class lessons, as part of a collaborative group, in pairs and individually.

11. Teachers recognising that the learning process and the acquisition of skills is at least as important as the learning of knowledge.

WEST GROVE PRIMARY SCHOOL
TEACHING AND LEARNING POLICY

12. Children having opportunities to create, express, enact, recount and communicate to others using a variety of media.

13. Recognising the importance of equal opportunities, taking account of special needs, gender, race, creed and class.

14. Having an approach which allows for differentiation in the curriculum to support both the less and more able, as well as those with special needs, in a sensitive manner.

15. At all stages recognising and planning appropriate assessment and record keeping systems that are used to guide future planning and ensure progression.

LEARNING

1. Pupils are entitled to have access to a wide range of learning materials, resources and 'real life' experiences.

2. Pupils are able to select materials and space in which to work, as appropriate to the task in hand.

3. Pupils are encouraged to take responsibility for caring for, organising and conserving learning resources in the classroom and school environment.

4. Pupils are given responsibility for organising and evaluating their learning and managing their own time.

5. The classroom and school environment will be used to reflect current work themes.

6. Both independent and co-operative work by pupils will be facilitated and encouraged.

7. Pupils should be encouraged to ask questions and to persevere.

8. Learning activities should be planned to enable progression and to allow children to experience success.

9. The atmosphere within the school should facilitate the development of good learning attitudes, which are appropriate in a variety of learning situations.

10. Pupil's specific individual interests should be valued and developed.

11. Pupils should understand that they, and the school, are parts of a wider community.

West Grove Primary School

Curriculum Planning and Delivery

This statement should be read in conjunction with the school's Curriculum Aim, the Aims of the school and the Teaching and Learning Policy.

West Grove Primary School recognises that the curriculum consists not only of the taught subjects but also the planned and incidental learning opportunities, which are available to pupils throughout the day.

Awareness of the individual needs of our pupils is central to effective curriculum planning and delivery. Learning opportunities are planned to ensure a match through differentiation and include class, group and individual teaching.

Taught time and Teaching day

At West Grove we consider all activities that take place within the school day have an educational element. They may not necessarily have specific objectives but structures and arrangements are in place for educational opportunities to be maximised throughout the day.

At present the school day is from 9.00am to 3.15pm. The main teaching sessions are as follows:

Nursery	Key Stage 1	Key Stage 2
9.00am – 11.30am	9.00am – 12.00pm	9.00am – 12.00pm
or	1.15pm – 3.15pm	1.00pm – 3.15pm
12.45pm – 3.15pm		
	Less 15mins assembly and 2 x 10mins playtime per day	Less 15mins assembly and 1 x 10mins playtime per day
Total: 2.5 hours per day	**Total: 4 hours 25 mins per day**	**Total: 4 hours 50 mins per day**

There are no set playtimes, as teachers and children decide when it is the right time for them to take a break – thus ending artificial breaks in learning. Playtime and lunchtime activities are planned in order to provide further opportunities for learning during those sessions. This also plays a part in the reduction of incidents of inappropriate behaviour during these sessions. The sessions are supervised by our Classroom Assistants in order to provide continuity of care.

Curriculum Planning

Our curriculum planning and delivery is being constructed in such a way as to prepare our pupils for the developing knowledge economy, which is being shaped by the following forces:

- Information and communication technologies
- Neuro-science, cognitive science and evolutionary psychology
- Work patterns and lifelong learning.

Creating a learning to learn school - research and practice for raising standards, motivation and morale

The knowledge and skills needed for the knowledge economy are:

- Meta-cognitive skills – thinking about how to think, learning how to learn
- Ability to integrate formal and informal learning
- Ability to access, select and evaluate knowledge in an information-soaked world
- Ability to develop and apply several forms of intelligence
- Ability to cope with ambiguous situations, unpredictable problems and unforeseeable circumstances
- Ability to cope with multiple careers, learning how to re-design oneself, locate oneself in a job market, choose and fashion the relevant education and training.

We have therefore taken this as the basis for our curriculum design.

Through our reading and research we have decided to deliver our curriculum through broad and balanced topics, which over the course of a year will take varied foci, e.g. science, history, geography, etc. We feel that, by learning and teaching through topics, it helps the children construct meaning within the real world and enables them to relate to and better understand their learning. It is through these topics that we deliver the National Curriculum and whenever possible draw links with the literacy and numeracy strategies. Where these links are not natural literacy and numeracy skills are taught separately.

Planning in Nursery and Reception classes is based on the Areas of Learning and the Early Learning Goals from the Curriculum Guidance for the foundation stage. We believe that these provide a sound basis for a high quality and integrated early education. The planning is based on observations of children's learning and is intended to support and extend that learning for each individual, who at several times across the foundation stage will be the subject of focus planning.

In order to build on this good early years' practice, we have considered many ways of planning and, in Key Stage 1, have used the nine areas of learning and experience (HMI 1985). We believe that these areas develop well from the early learning goals in the foundation stage, thereby enabling progression in skills as well as knowledge and understanding. We have since moved on in our thinking and from Autumn Term 2002 have started planning to VAKi in Key Stage 1 – planning opportunities for children to learn through visual, auditory and kinaesthetic experiences.

At the beginning of each topic the children in Key Stage 1 and Key Stage 2 are asked for their input through a brainstorm session. They are asked the following three questions:

- What do we already know about the topic?
- What do we want to know about the topic?
- How can we find out?

This is then referred to as the topic progresses so that the children are involved in the monitoring and evaluation of their own learning.

Curriculum Delivery

In order to maximise learning we are using several accelerated learning techniques, including:

- Brain gym
- VAKi

- Multiple intelligences
- Learning cycles
- Pulse learning
- Fruit and water available in classrooms
- Use of music
- Memory techniques.

Teachers are encouraged to develop their understanding of these techniques and use them as and when they feel appropriate throughout the day and/or week, although it is not possible to show them in weekly plans.

Weekly plans show the learning objectives for each area of learning and these form the basis of the focused teaching. This is then supplemented with individual or group activities for practice, etc.

Teachers are also assisting the children in developing their understanding of the learning techniques that they are developing, through discussion and feedback following observations.

Outdoor Environment

Opportunities should be provided, both formally and informally, for children to learn through the exploration of their environment.

This will include the use of the school grounds, the local community and trips further afield.

Creating a learning to learn school - *research and practice for raising standards, motivation and morale*

Finally, the following lists may prompt wider thinking about areas you might want to change or consider.

School-wide:

- culture and values
- community involvement
- parental involvement/family learning
- learning environment
- professional development and teacher constructs of ability
- use of coaches/mentors/TAs and other adults/peers
- policies, including school day, curriculum organization, planning frameworks, teaching and learning, use of data, assessment approaches, out of school learning
- use of resources, including ICT.

Classroom-level:

- the role of the teacher: team coach, explaining, commentating, orchestrating, modelling.
- having a model of learning: e.g. Ready, Go, Steady, Accelerated Learning Cycle
- learning styles: how information goes in (VAK)
- creativity: learning through different intelligences (MI)
- learning dispositions: knowing what to do when you get stuck, motivating yourself and setting goals, reviewing and improving
- understanding the mind's operating systems (and yourself as a learner): e.g. Brain Gym®, mind mapping, your ideal learning environment
- developing a language for expressing, relating and sharing 'learning to learn' experiences.

How will you implement the approach?

Think BIG, start small.

Elaine Wilmot, Headteacher, West Grove Primary School, London

Our 'learning to learn' approach is increasingly one of infusion. We started with a separate course, which can either be seen as the cuckoo in the nest or the catalyst for change. Staff need to see a model in action to understand and conceive it. It is a difficult concept to grasp without seeing it and making it visible.

Derek Wise, Headteacher, Cramlington Community High School, Northumberland

Having developed your vision, you must decide how to get there! As with all educational innovations there is no right or wrong way to develop 'learning to learn' in a school. Some of the project schools created new 'learning to learn' courses, some adopted 'learning to learn' in particular subject areas or with specific groups of pupils, some appointed a Head of Learning, while others provided INSET for all staff. While you will inevitably need to be flexible and change direction as events develop, having a sense of how you want to get to your desired destination is clearly important.

This section sets out a generalized model of the approach adopted by a majority of the project schools and highlights some of the important issues to be considered to ensure that staff development achieves its desired impact and does not dissipate when teachers are faced by the day to day reality of teaching the following day.

Professional development activity 2

Before looking at the project schools' model try the following professional development activity with the colleagues you worked with on the first mind map activity in this chapter where you discussed what has changed in your school over the past few years.

1. Talk about what helped and what hindered those changes.

2. What would you (either personally or as a school) do differently if you were faced by the same situation again?

3. Now think back to the vision or goal you have agreed for where you want to get to in the future.

4. Try to agree the single most important thing that you want to change in order to reach that vision.

5. What might help or hinder you?

6. Use photocopies of the research findings on pages 98 to 106 of this book as a discussion prompt with staff to assess how a 'learning to learn' approach might help you achieve your goal and what your own approach would need to involve.

7. Now focus on how you want to achieve that change using the chart on the previous page to consider the detailed areas and groups you will need to consider.

Creating a learning to learn school - research and practice for raising standards, motivation and morale

Area	What will it look like?	How will it be different?
Senior management		
Staff		
Pupils		
Parents		
The learning environment		
The curriculum		
The school day		
Assessment		
Governors		
Local community		
The LEA		
Other areas		

Developing 'learning to learn': the head's role

The following set of actions is based on the experiences of the 'learning to learn' project heads and provides a useful framework for activity to develop and implement a 'learning to learn' approach.

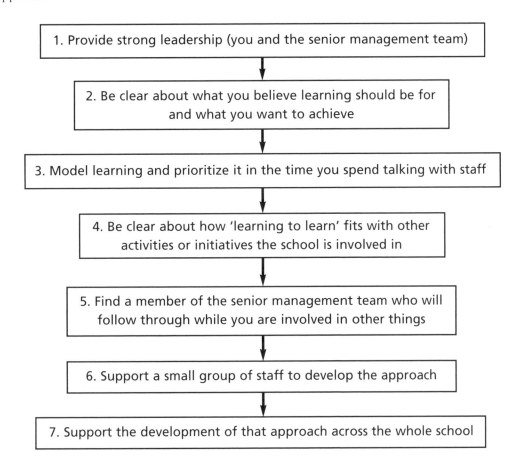

1. Provide strong leadership (you and the senior management team)

2. Be clear about what you believe learning should be for and what you want to achieve

3. Model learning and prioritize it in the time you spend talking with staff

4. Be clear about how 'learning to learn' fits with other activities or initiatives the school is involved in

5. Find a member of the senior management team who will follow through while you are involved in other things

6. Support a small group of staff to develop the approach

7. Support the development of that approach across the whole school

This model allows for huge variations in the actual approach adopted, with the main difference being around the nature of the small group of staff recruited to develop the approach and the specific objective given to them. Often, but not always, the group comprised a member of the senior management teacher, some experienced teachers and some younger staff. Most of the heads described the members of the group as 'pioneers' in some way, forward thinkers who could see the potential of 'learning to learn' and make it happen. The group was often made up of self-selected volunteers; one head had tried co-opting less positive staff onto the group, and although this had been effective in bringing them round to new ways of thinking, it had dissipated a lot of energy in the process.

Most groups were charged with developing a new syllabus as their objective, either for a newly created 'learning to learn' course or for a new way of teaching an existing course. The extent of this task inevitably defined the time and resources allocated to support their work, from virtually none at all to a specially timetabled meeting time and money to buy books, attend training and even study trips abroad.

As with most innovations, the key issue most heads encountered with 'learning to learn' was not initial development and delivery but the systematic rollout and implementation of the programme to other members of staff. One head suggested that, if he were starting out again, he would get all staff to develop a completely new skill and then reflect on how they had learned it, what had helped and hindered them, and what this might mean for the learning they provide in the classroom. The following sections set out some ideas on ensuring that CPD achieves its objectives and how structures can be used to embed 'learning to learn'.

Staff development for learning

Nothing has promised so much and has been so frustratingly wasteful as the thousands of workshops and conferences that led to no significant change in practice when the teachers returned to the classroom.

Michael Fullan, The New Meaning of Educational Change, 1991

As Michael Fullan indicates above, and you will know from your own experience, the real challenge in achieving change in schools lies in ensuring that staff CPD really changes practice.

This is dependent first and foremost on the development opportunities themselves embodying the learning principles that they espouse. Thus the learning process should:

- follow a clear model of learning;
- recognize and build on professionals' knowledge;
- provide the big picture and connect the learning through example;
- meet the needs of different learning styles;
- reflect brain/mind friendly principles, including through participative and collaborative activities;
- encourage learners to perform their understandings;
- include timely and formative feedback, including through peer coaching; and
- provide regular opportunities for review and reflection.

Creating a learning to learn school - *research and practice for raising standards, motivation and morale*

Modelling lifelong learning

Throughout this book the emphasis has been on schools developing lifelong learners and the need for heads and teachers to model learning themselves. Yet, too often, teachers are perceived by pupils as adults who have never left school. Equally, developing a learning culture among staff depends on trust and empathy, both of which are helped by a fuller understanding of people's lives and interests. Therefore, heads, teachers and other adults in schools should not only be seen to be learning professionally and modelling learning behaviours in the classroom, but should also be seen to be learning in the broadest sense - from and for life. For pupils to develop lifelong learning dispositions they must see learning as relevant to every sphere of life, from parenting, to holidays, to studying for further qualifications as an adult.

You could use the questions at the beginning of this book as the basis for staff discussions. Equally, despite all the pressure on time that is the reality of schools today, everything from secondments into industry to sabbaticals, and from staff book groups, to sessions in staff meetings when people talk about what they have learned outside school, occasional staff visits and outings and other opportunities to promote the value of life-wide learning, should all be encouraged.

Arguably, the role of the teacher as Team Coach outlined on page 76 provides an equally good model for any INSET provider. The difference with staff CPD is that it should combine both off-site workshops and ongoing practice and coaching within the classroom.

But high quality professional development of this type is only the first step in changing practice. American researchers Joyce and Showers have spent more than 20 years researching how to ensure that teachers translate newly learned teaching skills into long-term effective practice. They have identified four stages or components to the development (down the left-hand side of the diagram below) and the effect each one has on staff knowledge, skills and professional practice (along the top).

Component *training / coaching / performing* \ Impact *transforming*	Understanding the principles	Understanding the underlying theory	Consolidating the principles and developing the skills	Internalizing and applying to practice
(i) Exploration of theory through presentations / discussions / reading	███			
(ii) Demonstrations / modelling of skill(s)	░░░	░░░		
(iii) Simulated practice in 'workshop' with peer feedback	▓▓▓	▓▓▓	▓▓▓	
(iv) Peer coaching in 'workplace'	░░░	░░░	░░░	░░░

(Based on Joyce & Showers (op. cit.). Original concept by Professor Ray Bolam of Cardiff University)

What Joyce and Showers' research has shown is that, without steps three and four, even high quality INSET almost invariably makes no long-term impact on classroom practice. The implications for heads are clear.

Another very simple technique to ensure change happens on the back of an INSET session is to sit down with participants at the end and agree next steps by asking questions such as the following:

- Who will do what?
- Where do you want to be by the end of next week, this term and the school year?
- How you will monitor whether you have got there?

Making it stick

Having defined the vision, identified what needs to change and how they will achieve this, schools need to do more than provide inspirational INSET backed up with effective follow-up. Seeing 'learning to learn' through requires a persistent focus from the head and members of the SMT, but it also requires simple procedures and frameworks.

Derek Wise, headteacher at Cramlington Community High School in Northumberland has developed a highly successful school and 'learning to learn' approach. Teachers from the school now provide training and development at numerous national events and the school receives glowing Ofsted inspection reports for teaching and learning. Wise has written about his approach together with the school's Head of Science Mark Lovatt in *Creating an Accelerated Learning School* (see Resources section).

According to Wise 'The key thing is to integrate it with the planning framework, otherwise it's a bag of tricks with people not understanding why it works or how to repeat it next time'. An example of this systematic embedding of the approach has been the adoption of Alistair Smith's Accelerated Learning Cycle as a tool for planning all lessons. Cramlington has now developed this approach further with the loading of all lesson plans onto the school's intranet, so that supply staff can deliver them using interactive whiteboards if needed.

Many other excellent models and ideas for developing systems to support 'learning to learn' are included in *Leading the Learning School* by Colin Weatherley (see resources section). Weatherly organizes activity into the main headings of:

- collaborative culture: including leadership style and developing a cadre of staff to lead on school self-evaluation, policy development and implementation, peer coaching and communications (many of the 'learning to learn' schools adopted models of this type as the following sections explains); and

- development planning: including developing shared principles, such as a focus on teaching and learning, sharing the vision and reducing stress, and 'whole brain' planning.

PRE STAGE – CREATING THE SUPPORTIVE LEARNING ENVIRONMENT

- this does not happen by accident it is something the teacher actively plans to do

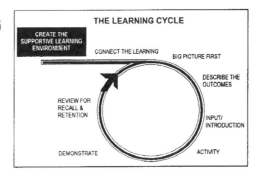

- ● **Welcome students into classroom e.g.**

  Smile
  Greet students positively
  Use "**we**" language i.e. "welcome to our classroom where today we are going to learn…"
  Make classroom a "**No Put Down Zone**"
  Use 3 positive strokes to every negative stroke
  Have high expectations of students
  Encourage a "**Can do/ will give it a go**" culture – tell them getting stuck is a good thing because it's a learning opportunity!

- ● **Do make sure your classroom is an exciting, stimulating, welcoming and tidy place to be**

  Arrange furniture and space to create a flexible learning environment
  Display students' work thoughtfully and creatively
  Use Keywords
  Make displays interactive
  Ensure surfaces are clear of clutter
  Use music to create atmosphere

- ● **Do beware of creating high stress situations**

  Eg: "Johnny can you tell me what you remember from last lesson…what do you mean you can't remember…it was only yesterday"

Much better to say

  "Ok in 1 minute I am going to ask you to tell me what you remember from last lesson…check in your notes and discuss with the person next to you what you remember…" – gives students the chance to check out what they are going to say

Figure 3.12.2 - from *Creating an Accelerated Learning School*, Network Educational Press Ltd, 2001

Conclusion

Given the right leadership by headteachers, senior managers and teachers, 'learning to learn' can be a very powerful way of improving the learning culture within a school. None of the teachers who took part in the first two phases of the 'learning to learn' project would claim that it is easy or that there is one blueprint which can be applied everywhere. 'Learning to learn' requires thought, planning and thorough understanding of the particular school context, but the benefits to teachers and students can be immense.

7 | Resources

Useful books

John Abbott and Terry Ryan, *The unfinished revolution: learning, human behaviour, community and political paradox*, Network Educational Press, 2000

Titus Alexander, *Citizenship Schools: a practical guide to education for citizenship and personal development*, Campaign for Learning, Southgate Publishers, 2001

Jackie Beere, *The Key Stage 3 learning toolkit*, Connect Publications, 2002

Paul Black and Dylan Wiliam, *Inside the black box*, King's College London, 1998

Paul Black et al, *Working inside the black box: assessment for learning in the classroom*, King's College London, 2002

Garry Burnett, *Learning to learn: making learning work for all students*, Crown House, 2002

Tony Buzan, *Use your head*, BBC Consumer Publishing, 2000

Renate Caine and Geoffrey Caine, *Unleashing the power of perceptual change*, ASCD, 1997

Rita Carter, *Mapping the mind*, Orion Fiction MMP, 2000

Guy Claxton, *Building Learning Power: helping young people become better learners*, TLO, 2002

Guy Claxton, *Hare brain, tortoise mind*, Fourth Estate, 1998

Guy Claxton, *Wise up, the challenge of lifelong learning*, Network Educational Press, 2000

Joseph O'Connor and Ian McDermott, *The principles of NLP*, Thorsons, 1996

Ruth Deakin Crick et al, *Testing, motivatin and learning*, Assessment Reform Group, 2002

Howard Gardner, *Frames of mind; the theory of multiple intelligences*, Basic Books, 1993

Daniel Goleman, *Emotional intelligence; why it matters more than IQ*, Bloomsbury, 1996

Susan Greenfield, *Brain story*, BBC Consumer Publishing, 2000

Susan Greenfield, *The private life of the brain*, John Wiley & Sons, 2001

Carla Hannaford, *Smart moves, why learning is not all in your head*, Great Ocean Publishers, 1995

Peter Honey and Alan Mumford, *The learning styles questionnaires; 80 item version*, Peter Honey Publications, 2000

Pierce Howard, *The owner's manual for the brain*, Bard Press, 2000

Mike Hughes, *Closing the learning gap*, Network Educational Press, 1999

Eric Jensen, *The learning brain*, The Brain Store Inc., 1995

Anne Kite, *A guide to better thinking: positive, critical, creative*, nferNelson, 2000

Bill Lucas, *Power up your mind; learn faster work smarter*, Nicholas Brealey Publishing Ltd, 2001

Bill Lucas & Toby Greany, *Schools in the learning age*, Southgate Publishers, 2000

Bill Lucas & Toby Greany, *Learning to learn: setting an agenda for schools in the 21st century*, Network Educational Press, 2001

Bill Lucas & Toby Greany, Jill Rodd and Ray Wicks, *Teaching pupils how to learn: research, practice and INSET resources*, Campaign for Learning, Network Educational Press, 2002

Carol McGuiness, *From thinking skills to thinking classrooms*, DfES, 1999

National Research Council (US), *How people learn; brain, mind, experience and the classroom*, National Academy Press, 2000

Mel Rockett and Simon Percival, Thinking for Learning, Network Educational Press, 2002

Jill Rodd, 'learning to learn' project research reports phases 1 and 2 available from www.campaign-for-learning.org.uk

Carl Rogers and Jerome Freiberg, *Freedom to learn,* Prentice Hall, 1994

Colin Rose and Malcolm Nicholl, *Accelerated learning for the 21st century,* Piatkus Books, 1997

Martin Seligman, *Learned optimism: how to change your mind and your life,* Pocket Books, 1998

Peter Senge et al., *Schools that learn,* Nicholas Brealey Publishing Ltd, 2000

Alistair Smith, *Accelerated learning in the classroom*, Network Educational Press, 1996

Alistair Smith, *Accelerated learning in practice*, Network Educational Press, 1998

Alistair Smith and Nicola Call, *The ALPS approach resource book*, Network Educational Press, 2001

Transforming the way we learn: a vision for the future of ICT in schools, DfES, 2002

Colin Weatherley, *Leading the learning school,* Network Educational Press, 2000

Derek Wise and Mark Lovatt, *Creating an accelerated learning school*, Network Educational Press, 2001

Other resources

Assessment Reform Group, *Assessment for Learning*

Learning to learn in schools: Phase 1 project Research Report, Dr Jill Rodd (available from www.campaign-for-learning.org.uk)

Teaching and Learning Research Programme (ESRC) *Newsletters*

Useful web sites

www.alite.co.uk – Alistair Smith's Accelerated Learning site

www.campaign-for-learning.org.uk – the Campaign for Learning's site

www.learntolearn.org – CHAMPS, the first online learning to learn course developed by Accelerated Learning Systems with the Campaign

www.21learn.org – the 21st Century Learning Initiaitve site

www.networkpress.co.uk – Publishers of many learning to learn books

www.accelerated-learning.co.uk – distributors of many learning to learn books

www.ex.ac.uk/ESRC-TLRP/ - the ESRC Teaching and Learning Research Programme site

www.standards.dfes.gov.uk – the DfES Standards and Effectiveness Unit site, including the Teaching and Learning in Foundation Subjects (TLF) Key Stage 3 strand

Appendix

The project's patrons: Professor Tim Brighouse, Sir John Daniel, Professor Susan Greenfield and Professor David Hargreaves

The project's advisory board: John Abbott, Dr Javier Bajer, Sir Christopher Ball, Tom Bentley, Dr Chris Brookes, Tony Buzan, Jose Chambers, Professor Guy Claxton, Galina Dolya, Neil Dunnicliffe, Maggie Farrah, Dr Peter Honey, Jim Houghton, Lesley James, Professor Elizabeth Leo, Dr Bill Lucas, Dr Juliet Merrifield, Roger Opie, Colin Rose, Judy Sebba, Alistair Smith, Lady Mary Tovey, Ray Wicks and Kate Williamson

Index

Creating a learning to learn school - *research and practice for raising standards, motivation and morale*

Other NEP Publications

THE SCHOOL EFFECTIVENESS SERIES

Book 1:   *Accelerated Learning in the Classroom* by Alistair Smith
ISBN: 1-85539-034-5

Book 2:   *Effective Learning Activities* by Chris Dickinson
ISBN: 1-85539-035-3

Book 3:   *Effective Heads of Department* by Phil Jones and Nick Sparks
ISBN: 1-85539-036-1

Book 4:   *Lessons are for Learning* by Mike Hughes
ISBN: 1-85539-038-8

Book 5:   *Effective Learning in Science* by Paul Denley and Keith Bishop
ISBN: 1-85539-039-6

Book 6:   *Raising Boys' Achievement* by Jon Pickering
ISBN: 1-85539-040-X

Book 7:   *Effective Provision for Able and Talented Children* by Barry Teare
ISBN: 1-85539-041-8

Book 8:   *Effective Careers Education and Guidance* by Andrew Edwards and Anthony Barnes   ISBN: 1-85539-045-0

Book 9:   *Best behaviour and Best behaviour FIRST AID* by Peter Relf, Rod Hirst, Jan Richardson and Georgina Youdell   ISBN: 1-85539-046-9

               Best behaviour FIRST AID
ISBN: 1-85539-047-7 (pack of 5 booklets)

Book 10: *The Effective School Governor* by David Marriott
ISBN 1-85539-042-6 (including free audio tape)

Book 11: *Improving Personal Effectiveness for Managers in Schools*
by James Johnson   ISBN 1-85539-049-3

Book 12: *Making Pupil Data Powerful* by Maggie Pringle and Tony Cobb
ISBN 1-85539-052-3

Book 13: *Closing the Learning Gap* by Mike Hughes
ISBN 1-85539-051-5

Book 14: *Getting Started* by Henry Leibling
ISBN 1-85539-054-X

Book 15: *Leading the Learning School* by Colin Weatherley
ISBN 1-85539-070-1

Book 16: *Adventures in Learning* by Mike Tilling
ISBN 1-85539-073-6

Book 17: *Strategies for Closing the Learning Gap*

by Mike Hughes and Andy Vass   ISBN 1-85539-075-2

Book 18: *Classroom Management* by Phillip Waterhouse and Chris Dickinson

ISBN 1-85539-079-5

Book 19: *Effective Teachers* by Tony Swainston

ISBN 1-85539-125-2

Book 20: *Transforming Teaching and Learning* by Colin Weatherley, Bruce Bonney, John Kerr and Jo Morrison

ISBN 1-85539-080-9

ACCELERATED LEARNING SERIES

General Editor: **Alistair Smith**

Accelerated Learning in Practice by Alistair Smith   ISBN 1-85539-048-5

The ALPS Approach: Accelerated Learning in Primary Schools

by Alistair Smith and Nicola Call   ISBN 1-85539-056-6

MapWise by Oliver Caviglioli and Ian Harris

ISBN 1-85539-059-0

The ALPS Approach Resource Book by Alistair Smith and Nicola Call

ISBN 1-85539-078-7

Creating an Accelerated Learning School by Mark Lovatt and Derek Wise

ISBN 1-85539-074-4

ALPS StoryMaker by Stephen Bowkett   ISBN 1-85539-076-0

Thinking for Learning by Mel Rockett and Simon Percival   ISBN 1-85539-096-5

Reaching out to all learners by Cheshire LEA   ISBN 1-85539-143-0

Leading Learning by Alistair Smith   ISBN 1-85539-089-2

Bright Sparks by Alistair Smith   ISBN 1-85539-088-4

Move It by Alistair Smith   ISBN 1-85539-123-6

EDUCATION PERSONNEL MANAGEMENT SERIES

Education Personnel Management handbooks help headteachers, senior managers and governors to manage a broad range of personnel issues.

The Well Teacher – management strategies for beating stress, promoting staff health and reducing absence by Maureen Cooper   ISBN 1-85539-058-2

Managing Challenging People – dealing with staff conduct

by Bev Curtis and Maureen Cooper   ISBN 1-85539-057-4

Managing Poor Performance – handling staff capability issues

by Bev Curtis and Maureen Cooper   ISBN 1-85539-062-0

Managing Allegations Against Staff – personnel and child protection issues in schools by Maureen Cooper and Bev Curtis   ISBN 1-85539-072-8

Managing Recruitment and Selection – appointing the best staff

by Maureen Cooper and Bev Curtis   ISBN 1-85539-077-9

Managing Redundancies – dealing with reduction and reorganisation of staff by Maureen Cooper and Bev Curtis   ISBN 1-85539-082-5

Managing Pay in Schools – performance management and pay in schools

by Bev Curtis   ISBN 1-85539-087-6

VISIONS OF EDUCATION SERIES

The Unfinished Revolution by John Abbott and Terry Ryan   ISBN 1-85539-064-7

The Learning Revolution by Jeannette Vos and Gordon Dryden   ISBN 1-85539-085-X

Wise Up by Guy Claxton   ISBN 1-85539-099-X

ABLE AND TALENTED CHILDREN COLLECTION

Effective Resources for Able and Talented Children by Barry Teare

ISBN 1-85539-050-7

More Effective Resources for Able and Talented Children by Barry Teare

ISBN 1-85539-063-9

Challenging Resources for Able and Talented Children by Barry Teare

ISBN 1-85539-122-8

MODEL LEARNING

Thinking Skills And Eye Q by Oliver Caviglioli, Ian Harris and Bill Tindall

ISBN 1-85539-091-4

Class Maps by Oliver Caviglioli and Ian Harris

ISBN 1-85539-139-2

OTHER TITLES

The Thinking Child by Nicola Call with Sally Featherstone   ISBN 1-85539-121-X

Becoming Emotionally Intelligent by Catherine Corrie   ISBN 1-85539-069-8

That's Science by Tim Harding   ISBN 1-85539-170-8

The Brain's Behind It by Alistair Smith   ISBN 1-85539-083-3

Help Your Child To Succeed by Bill Lucas and Alistair Smith   ISBN 1-85539-111-2

Tweak to Transform by Mike Hughes   ISBN 1-85539-140-6

Brain Friendly Revision by UFA National Team   ISBN 1-85539-127-9

Numeracy Activities Key Stage 2 by Afzal Ahmed and Honor Williams
ISBN 1-85539-102-3

Numeracy Activities Key Stage 3 by Afzal Ahmed, Honor Williams and
George Wickham   ISBN 1-85539-103-1

Teaching Pupils How to Learn by Bill Lucas, Toby Greany, Jill Rodd and Ray Wicks
ISBN 1-85539-098-1

Basics for School Governors by Joan Sallis   ISBN 1-85539-012-4

Imagine That... by Stephen Bowkett   ISBN 1-85539-043-4

Self-Intelligence by Stephen Bowkett   ISBN 1-85539-055-8

Class Talk by Rosemary Sage   ISBN 1-85539-061-2

Creating a learning to learn school - *research and practice for raising standards, motivation and morale*